STUDENT STUDY GUIDE

to accompany

Creating Inclusive Classrooms
Effective and Reflective Practices

Fourth Edition

Spencer J. Salend

Prepared by
Laurel Garrick Duhaney

Upper Saddle River, New Jersey
Columbus, Ohio

10 9 8 7 6 5 4 3 2

Merrill
Prentice Hall

ISBN: 0-13-090014-1

Table of Contents

About This *Student Study Guide*

This *Student Study Guide* has been designed to enhance your understanding of the information presented in the text, *Creating Inclusive Classrooms: Effective and Reflective Practices*. Each chapter of the textbook has a corresponding chapter in the *Student Study Guide* that includes the following:

- Chapter Overview
- Chapter Objectives
- Outline
- Chapter Summary
- Key Terms
- Learning Activities
- Guided Review
- Application Exercises
- Reflective Exercises
- Informational Section

In addition, a self-test consisting of multiple-choice, true or false, sentence completion, matching, and essay questions has been included in the study guide. Varied test formats have been used in this study guide to help you perform your best. Moreover, the self-tests have been designed to measure your higher-level and lower-level learning. Each chapter includes items that test your knowledge, comprehension, application, analysis, synthesis, and evaluation of the information presented in the text. Answers for the self-tests are provided at the end of the student study guide. The pages where the answers to the multiple-choice, true or false, sentence completion, and matching questions can be found are also provided.

Here are some tips that can help you take the self-tests.

- Go through the test once and answer all the questions you can.
- Go through the test again. If you can, answer the questions you missed the first time. Don't spend too much time on a question if you find it difficult. Move on.
- Double-check your answers at the end and make sure you haven't made any clerical errors.

You will find the *Student Study Guide* most beneficial if used in the following way:
- Carefully read your instructor's course calendar or schedule for the sequence of course topics, the preparations or readings, and the assignments, term papers, and examinations due. Consider the nature of the course competencies. For example, determine whether the examinations will be multiple-choice, essays, short answers,

take-home tests, etc. This will help you budget your time and structure your academic efforts.

- Maybe you, like most students, are worried about taking examinations. Yet you
- realize that examinations give important information such as the course
- objectives you have mastered and the topics and skills that you still need to learn.

Notwithstanding these benefits, test taking also is emotionally laden and anxiety producing. The following strategies can help you lessen the anxiety surrounding test-taking.

1. After you have read each chapter in your text, use the chapter outline and summary in this study guide to assist you in organizing your notes.
2. Review each subtopic in the chapter outline and see how much information you can recall about the topic. If you can't remember anything, reread the information.
3. After you have reviewed the information in each chapter, take the chapter test. Be sure to read the instructions and test items carefully. Check your score, review the information you have not yet mastered, and retake the entire test. This will give you a chance to reinforce what you have learned.

Chapter 1: Understanding Inclusion

Chapter Overview

Chapter one introduces the concept of inclusion, the philosophical principles that guide this book, and factors that contributed to the growth of inclusion. The chapter begins with a vignette that illustrates the disparate experiences of two families and their children with disabilities. The issues and events that impact the lives of these, and other students with disabilities and their families, are examined in light of such principles as inclusion, the least restrictive environment, mainstreaming, and legal mandates that shaped special education. Chapter one also discusses issues related to the challenges of implementing inclusion as well as its impact on students with and without disabilities, their teachers, and their families.

Chapter Objectives

Upon completion of this chapter, students should be able to:

1. Define the concepts of inclusion, mainstreaming, and the least restrictive environment.
2. Discuss the differences and similarities among the concepts of inclusion, mainstreaming, and the least restrictive environment.
3. Describe the factors that contributed to the movement to educate students in inclusive classrooms.
4. Discuss laws that affected special education.
5. Describe the impact of inclusion on students with disabilities, students without disabilities, their educators, and their families.

Chapter Outline

I. *Mary and Marie* (Chapter-opening vignette)
II. What Is Inclusion?
    1. Inclusion
    2. Principles of Effective Inclusion
       a. Diversity
       b. Individual Needs

       c. Reflective Practice

       d. Collaboration

       e. Mainstreaming

III.   What Is the Least Restrictive Environment?

    1.   Least Restrictive Environment

    2.   Continuum of Educational Placements

       a. General Education Classroom Placement with Few or No Supportive Services

       b. General Education Placement with Collaboration Teacher Assistance

       c. General Education Classroom Placement with Itinerant Specialist Assistance

       d. General Education Classroom Placement with Resource Room Assistance

       e. Special Education Classroom Placement with Part-Time in the General Education Classroom

       f. Full-Time Special Education Classroom

       g. Special Day School

       h. Residential School

       i. Homebound instruction

       j. Hospital or Institution

IV.   What Factors Contributed to the Movement to Educate Students in Inclusive Classrooms?

    1.   Normalization

    2.   Deinstitutionalization

    3.   Early Intervention and Early Childhood Programs

    4.   Technological Advances

    5.   Civil Rights Movement and Resulting Litigation

       a. *Brown v. Topeka Board of Education*

       b. *Pennsylvania Association for Retarded Children v. Commonwealth of Pennsylvania*

       c. *Mills v. Board of Education of the District of Columbia*

       d. *Hobsen v. Hanson*

       e. *Diana v. California State Board of Education*

       f. *Lau v. Nichols*

       g. *Larry P. v. Riles*

       h. *Board of Education of the Hendrick Hudson School District v. Rowley*

       i. *Irving Independent School District v. Tatro*

       j. *Timothy W. v. Rochester, N.H. School District*

       k. *Agostini v. Felton*

       l. *Cedar Rapids Community School District v. Garrett F.*

    6.   Advocacy Groups

    7.   Segregated nature of Special Schools and Classes

    8.   Disproportionate Representation

Chapter Summary

Chapter one highlighted some of the fundamentals of inclusion as well as reflections on professional practices for implementing inclusion. Factors that contributed toward the momentum for inclusion were described, and significant laws that shaped special education were discussed. Research on the impact of inclusion on students with and without disabilities, their educators, and their families was presented.

Key Terms

The following are important concepts from this chapter. Using the information in the chapter, write your own definition. If you think and write (actively process the information), as opposed to quoting the information from the chapter (passively process the information), you will remember the information better.

Inclusion	Disproportional representation
Mainstreaming	Disparate treatment
Least restrictive environment	Individuals with Disabilities Education Act (IDEA)
Continuum of educational placements	IDEA Amendments of 1997
Americans with Disabilities Act	Education for All Handicapped Children Act (EAHCA)
Normalization	EAHCA Amendments of 1896
Deinstitutionalization	Individualized Family Service Plan
Section 504 of the Rehabilitation Act	Tech Act
Disparate impact	Advocacy groups
Early intervention and early childhood programs	

Learning Activities

1. Read the vignette *Reflections on Professional Practice: Implementing Inclusion.* Generate a list of at least ten questions to ask educators who teach in an inclusive education classroom. Get permission to visit and observe an inclusive education classroom in your school district. Try to get answers to the survey you have devised. Write up your observations and discuss your findings with the class. You should also visit a mildly integrated setting (i.e., a special education classroom within a public school building) and a highly segregated setting (e.g., special day school, residential program, hospital, institution). Ask the educators in these settings similar questions to the ones on the list you have developed. To get you started, some questions to ask may include:

a. What types of students are in this classroom?

b. Which professionals work in an instructional capacity with these students?

c. What are the roles and responsibilities of each professional?

d. How is the curriculum organized? (e.g., by subject area, theme)

e. What are the educational goals of the setting?

f. What modifications have been made to accommodate the range of abilities and disabilities in the class?

g. How is instruction assessed?

2. Create a survey to assess the definitions and opinions of local general education teachers, special education teachers, and family members of children with and without disabilities concerning inclusion. Record the responses and share the findings with the class. As responses are shared, compare and contrast the definitions of inclusion. In discussing the opinions of each group, highlight the variations in their perceptions regarding the impact of inclusion.

3. Interview personnel from your local school district who are responsible for the implementation of inclusion. Find out how schools are held accountable for complying with the policies. Discuss your findings with the class. The interview questions could include:

a. What students with disabilities are educated in general education classrooms?

b. Who is responsible for coordinating the district's inclusion and mainstreaming programs?

c. What are the procedures to prepare students with disabilities for entry into general education classes?

d. What are the procedures for preparing students without disabilities for the entry of students with disabilities into their classes?

e. Does the district have procedures for establishing communication and consultation between educators and with families? If so, what are they?

f. Does the district offer inservice training programs on inclusion related topics? If so, of what does the training consist?

g. How does the district assess student progress in general education settings?

h. What problems has the district encountered in implementing inclusion?

i. What solutions has the district developed to address these problems?

j. What system of accountability is in place to ensure that school districts are in compliance with inclusion policies? What are the consequences for noncompliance?

4. Discuss ways in which the normalization principle has been implemented and could be more fully implemented in your local community and society.

5. Discuss the following:

a. Do you have a relative or neighbor who has a disability?

b. How has knowing this individual affected your views of individuals with disabilities?

c. How has that individual affected you and others in your family and neighborhood?

d. Have you developed a friendship with this individual? Why or why not?

e. What are some benefits to this friendship? Alternatively, what are some factors that prevent the development of a friendship?

6. Attend meetings of a local advocacy group and/or serve as an advocate for a student with a disability.

7. Debate the proposition: Inclusion and Mainstreaming Benefit Students, Schools, and Society. Structure the debate so that each debating team comprises individuals who will debate the proposition from the perspective of special educators, general educators, school administrators, students with disabilities, students who are not disabled, parents of students with disabilities, parents of students who are not disabled, and educational researchers. For example, both teams would have a special educator debate the proposition. The special educator on the team that supports the proposition would argue for it from the special educator's perspective, while the special educator on the team that is against the proposition would argue against it. One good source to get you started with information for the debate is Stainback, W., & Stainback, S. (1996), *Controversial issues confronting special education: Divergent perspectives* (5ᵗʰ ed.). Boston, MA: Allyn & Bacon.

8. Summarize the findings of five articles that discuss the disproportionate representation of students from culturally and linguistically diverse backgrounds in special education.

9. Interview a local school administrator regarding the provision of services under Section 504 of the Rehabilitation Act. You may choose to ask the administrator the following questions, modify the questions, or develop your own questions.

a. Would you prefer a student to be eligible under the IDEA or Section 504? Why or why not?

b. What groups of students receive services under Section 504?

c. What is the nature of the services that they receive?

d. Once students are identified for services, do they always receive them? What are reasons for suspension and/or termination of services?

Guided Review

Chapter opening vignette, *Marie and Mary*

1. Compare and contrast the school and community experiences of Marie and Mary.

_____

_____

2. Describe the factors and events that led to the differential experiences of Marie, Mary, and their families in school and society.

_____

_____

3. Why are the outcomes so different for Mary and her family?

_____

_____

After reading this chapter, you should be able to answer these as well as the following questions.

a. What is inclusion?
b. What is the least restrictive environment?
c. What factors contributed to the movement to educate students in inclusive classrooms?

What Is Inclusion?

4. Define inclusion.

_____

_____

5. Identify and describe the four principles of inclusion.

Name of Principle	Description

6. The vignette "Reflections on Professional Practices" describes an inclusive classroom. Read the vignette, then answer these questions.

a. What aspects of their school day and program make you believe that Ms. Silver, Mr. Thomas, and Ms. Williams address the educational, social, and behavioral needs of their students?

b. What roles did Ms. Silver, Mr. Thomas, Ms. Williams, and their students play in their classroom?

c. How did Ms. Silver, Mr. Thomas, and Ms. Williams address the educational, social, and behavioral needs of their students?

d. What types of support services do Ms. Silver and Ms. Williams receive to help them implement their program?

e. What types of support do educators need to implement an inclusion program?

Mainstreaming

7. What is mainstreaming? How is mainstreaming different from inclusion?

_____

_____

What Is the Least Restrictive Environment?

8. What does the least restrictive environment concept mean?

    _____

    _____

    _____

9. List and briefly describe the range of placements from most to least restrictive setting for students with disabilities.

    _____

    _____

    _____

10. Your textbook summarizes five judicial decisions that school districts should consider in placing a student with a disability in the least restrictive environment. What are these decisions?

    a. _____

        _____

    b. _____

        _____

    c. _____

        _____

    d. _____

        _____

    e. _____

        _____

What Factors Contributed to the Movement to Educate Students in Inclusive Classrooms?

11. List the nine factors that contributed to the movement to educate students in inclusive classrooms as presented in your textbook.

    _____

    _____

    _____

12. What is the normalization principle?

    _____

    _____

13. What is the deinstitutionalization principle?

_____

_____

_____

14. What are the benefits of early intervention and early childhood programs?

_____

_____

_____

15. List five characteristics of early intervention programs.

_____

_____

_____

16. Describe how technological advances have promoted the mainstreaming movement.

_____

_____

17. Discuss the major outcomes of these cases.

a. *Brown v. Topeka Board of Education*
b. *Pennsylvania Association for Retarded Children v. Commonwealth of Pennsylvania*
c. *Mills v. Board of Education of the District of Columbia*
d. *Hobsen v. Hansen*
e. *Diana v. California State Board of Education*
f. *Lau v. Nichols*
g. *Larry P. v. Riles*
h. *Board of Education of the Hendrick Hudson School District v. Rowley*
i. *Irving Independent School District v. Tatro*
k. *Timothy W. v. Rochester, N.H. School District*
l. *Agostini v. Felton*
m. *Cedar Rapids Community School District v. Garrett F.*

18. How have advocacy groups contributed to the inclusion movement?

_____

_____

19. Explain why Lloyd Dunn questioned the segregation of students with mild disabilities.

_____

_____

20. What did the research on the effectiveness of special education programs reveal?

a.

b.

c.

21. List ten factors that promote school dropout.

a.   b.

c.   d.

e.   f.

g.   h.

i.   j.

22. How does Yates define disproportionate representation?

_____
_____
_____

23. Provide two examples of disparate treatment in school.

a.

b.

24. Cite two examples of disparate impact in school.

a.

b.

25. What is a major challenge that schools face in attempting to reform the educational system?

_____
_____

26. The reauthorized Individuals with Disabilities Education Act specifies that school

districts and state departments of education must determine if the problems of overrepresentation and underrepresentation exist, as well as the nature of these problems. List a minimum of five of the questions presented in your textbook that can be used to evaluate the extent to which students in your school district are disproportionately represented.

a. _____
b. _____
c. _____
d. _____
e. _____

What Are the Laws That Shaped Special Education?

27. What does the "IDEA" stand for?

_____

28. List the ten components of the Individualized Family Service Plan.

a.   f.
b.   g.
c.   h.
d.   i.
e.   j.

29. List the major provisions of the IDEA of 1997 (PL 105-17) as presented in your textbook.

a.

b.

c

d.

e.

f .

g.

h.

i.

j.

k.

30. According to the text, the IDEA is based on six fundamental principles that govern the education of students with disabilities. Using the following table, write out the name of each principle and the major characteristic of the principle.

Name of Principle	Major Characteristic
a.	
b.	
c.	
d.	
e.	
f.	

31. Beginning with the earliest to the latest amendment, give the number, name, and major concepts of the four amendments to the IDEA as listed in your textbook.

Number of Law	Name of Law	Major Concept
a.		
b.		
c.		
d.		

Other Laws Affecting Special Education

32. List two other federal laws that affect special education and students with disabilities.

a.

b.

33. What are major provisions of Section 504 of the Rehabilitation Act?

_____

_____

_____

34. Identify some of the similarities and differences between the IDEA and Section 504 of the Rehabilitation Act.

_____

_____

_____

_____

_____

35. Identify two of the major provisions of the American with Disabilities Act.

_____

_____

_____

_____

What Is the Impact of Inclusion?

36. Research reveals that the impact of inclusion on students with and without disabilities, teachers and parents is varied. Provide at least two points on the impact of inclusion for each of these groups.

Impact of Inclusion on Students with Disabilities

a. Academic Performance:

b. Social Performance:

c. Attitudes Toward Placement:

Impact of Inclusion on Students Without Disabilities

a. Academic Performance:

b. Social Performance:

Impact of Inclusion on Educators

a. Attitudes Toward Inclusion:

b. Outcomes for General Educators:

c. Outcomes for Special Educators:

Impact of Inclusion on Families

a. Families of Children with Disabilities:

b. Families of Children Without Disabilities:

Application Exercise for Chapter 1

Read "What Would You Do in Today's Diverse Classroom?" and answer the following questions.

a. How would you answer a family member who said, "I'm all for having a variety of students in the class, but won't students with special needs take time away from the other kids?"

b. What other questions do you think families might have about inclusion?
c. What can teachers do to help family members understand inclusion programs and build support among families for inclusion?

Reflective Exercises for Chapter 1

1. Some advocates of inclusion see the use of options as a deterrent to educating students in general education classrooms because it helps to maintain a dual system of general and special education. Others think that the continuum of placements recognizes the diverse needs of students and the different environments that can be used to address these needs. What is your view?

2. Technological and medical advances have had a far-reaching impact on ALL members of society. For example, Alexander Graham Bell's attempts to amplify his voice so that he could improve his communication with his wife, who had a hearing impairment, led to the invention of the telephone (Blanck, 1994). What technological devices do you use?

3. Think of a relative, friend, or neighbor who has a disability. How has that individual affected you and others in your family and neighborhood?

4. The issues of disproportionality are not only multifaceted but are shaped by the cultural experiences of students and professionals. As a result, educators should examine whether their policies, practices, attitudes, and behaviors result in disparate treatment and disparate impact for students from culturally and linguistically diverse backgrounds.

a. Can you think of other examples of disparate treatment and disparate impact in schools? In society?

b. How would you rate the extent to which disproportional representation exists in your school district? ( ) Doesn't Exist ( ) Exists to Some Extent ( ) Exists Extensively

c. What are some goals and steps your school district can adopt to address disproportional representation?

5. By replacing the term *handicapped* with the term *disabilities* in the IDEA, Congress recognized the importance of language. What do the terms *regular, normal,* and *special* imply? How do these terms affect the ways we view students with disabilities and the programs designed to meet their needs? Do these terms foster inclusion or segregation?

6. Some educators propose that teachers should be allowed to decide whether to work in a setting that includes students with disabilities. Do you think teachers should have a choice about the types of students they teach? Now ask yourself, should teachers be given a choice about the academic levels, ethnic, linguistic, and religious backgrounds, socioeconomic status, gender, and sexual orientation of the students they teach? If you were given such a choice, what types of students would you include? Exclude?

7. If you were a family member of a child with a disability, would you prefer a general or special education setting? If you were a family member of a child who was not disabled, would you prefer an inclusion class?

For Your Information

1. Volume 19, number 4 of Remedial and Special Education (1998) presents a history of the treatment and education of children and adults with disabilities.

2. Salend and Duhaney (1999) provide a summary of the research with respect to inclusion programs and students with and without disabilities, and their teachers.

3. Blazer (1999) offers tips for developing Section 504 classroom accommodation plan.

SELF-TEST FOR CHAPTER 1

Directions: Select the best answer for each question. Try to answer each question, even though you might be unsure of the best answer. Remember that this is a practice test. You will not be penalized for guessing. However, before you take your class examinations, you should clarify with the instructor whether you will be penalized for guessing.

Multiple Choice Questions

1. Which of the following best characterizes inclusive practices?
   a. Reintegrate families and community members to foster schools based on acceptance
   b. Incorporate the principles of diversity, individual needs, reflective practice, and collaboration
   c. Bring together students and educators in mainstreamed settings
   d. Built on competitive, consultative, accommodating, responsive teacher and student relationships

2. Which of the following best describes the least restrictive environment within the continuum of educational placements?
   a. General education classroom placement with few or no supportive services
   b. General education classroom placement with collaboration teacher assistance
   c. General education classroom placement with itinerant specialist assistance
   d. General education classroom with few or no supportive services

3. Which of the following is **not** a role of the resource room teacher?
   a. Helps general education teachers provide indirect services to students with disabilities
   b. Provides individualized remedial instruction in specific skills
   c. Provides supplemental instruction that parallels the instruction in general education classrooms
   d. Assists general classroom teachers in planning and implementing instructional modifications for students

4. Early intervention and early childhood programs have:
   a. Disempowered families to promote their child's educational development.
   b. Reduced the likelihood that secondary disabilities will occur.
   c. Decreased the probability that children with disabilities will be socially independent.
   d. Decreased the likelihood that children with disabilities will be financially secure.

5. The precedent for much special education-related litigation was:
    a. *Brown v. Topeka Board of Education*
    b. *Mill v. Board of Education of the District of Columbia*
    c. *Hobsen v. Hanson*
    d. *Diana v. California State Board of Education*

6. In *Agostini v. Felton*, the Supreme Court stated that:
    a. No matter how severe a student's disability is or how little a student may benefit, the school must educate the student.
    b. Tracking was unconstitutional and should be abolished, as it segregated students on the basis of race and/or economic status.
    c. School districts may provide on-site special education and related services to students attending religious schools .
    d. PL 94-142 was designed to provide students with disabilities with reasonable opportunities to learn.

7. This individual argued that special education classes for students with mild disabilities were unjustifiable because they were a form of homogeneous grouping and tracking.
    a. Chief Justice Earl Warren
    b. Evelyn Deno
    c. Lloyd Dunn
    d. Madeline Will

8. Treating all students similarly is:
    a. Disparate impact.
    b. Disparate treatment.
    c. Disproportionate representation.
    d. Disproportionality.

9. This law authorizes schools to provide Mary, a student with profound mental retardation, free and appropriate educational services.
    a. Americans with Disabilities Act
    b. Individuals with Disabilities Education Act
    c. Rehabilitation Act
    d. Family Educational Rights and Privacy Act

10. The zero reject principle of the IDEA states that all students with disabilities must:
    a. Be included in schools.
    b. Be educated in the general education classroom.
    c. Receive equal education to that of their peers who are not disabled.
    d. Receive quality education in special education classrooms.

11. This Act included provisions for infants, toddlers, and preschoolers, and encouraged early intervention services.
    a. PL 99-457
    b. PL 94-142
    c. PL 101-476
    d. PL 105-17

12. This is **not** a major provision of the IDEA Amendments of 1997:
    a. Disproportionate representation
    b. Fiscal policies
    c. Participation in assessments
    d. Discipline

13. Research on the effects of inclusion on educators suggests that:
    a. They generally agree with the placement of students with disabilities in general education classrooms.
    b. Some are satisfied with a pull-out system for delivering special education services.
    c. Middle and high school teachers appear to favor inclusion less than elementary teachers.
    d. All of the above.

14. Research on the significance of inclusion to families suggests that:
    a. Families of children with and without disabilities share similar perspectives on inclusion.
    b. Families of children with disabilities are concerned about the loss of individualized special education services.
    c. Families of children without disabilities feel that an inclusive classroom does not prevent their children from receiving a good education.
    d. Some families are concerned about their child being educated with children with physical and sensory disabilities.

True or False Questions

Directions: Read each statement carefully. Circle true if the answer is true, and false if the answer is false.

15. Both mainstreaming and inclusion have their roots in the concept of the least restrictive environment.
    True   False

16. The determination of the least restrictive environment is based on a student's educational need rather than a student's disability.
    True   False

17. A student with a disability can only be placed in a more restrictive setting when he or she cannot be educated satisfactorily in the general education classroom.
    True   False

18. Assistive technology only has consequences and benefits for students with disabilities.
    True   False

19. PL 94-142, The Education of All Handicapped Children Act, was renamed the Individuals with Disabilities Education Act.
    True   False

20. The least restrictive environment concept means that all students with disabilities should be educated in general education classrooms.
    True   False

21. Itinerant teachers often travel from school to school to provide services to students.
    True   False

22. In 1990, Congress passed the Individuals with Disabilities Education Act, which expanded the categories of students with disabilities to include Attention Deficit Disorders.
    True   False

23. Section 504 of the Rehabilitation Act employs a narrower definition of disabilities than the disability categories covered under the Individuals with Disabilities Education Act.
    True   False

24. Students with attention deficit disorders are potential recipients of services under Section 504 of the Rehabilitation Act.
    True   False

Sentence Completion Questions

25. The process of moving individuals with disabilities from large institutional settings to smaller community-based independent living arrangements is called _____.

26. _____ seeks to establish collaborative, supportive, and nurturing communities of learners that are based on giving all students the services and accommodations they need to learn.

27. The principle of _____ seeks to provide social interactions and experiences that parallel those of society to adults and children with disabilities.

28. The *Brown v. Topeka Board of Education* case of 1954 established the principle of _____.

29. Both mainstreaming and inclusion are rooted in the concept of the _____.

Essay Questions

30. Define mainstreaming, inclusion, and the least restrictive environment. Discuss how these are related and how they differ.

31. Identify and discuss the four principles on which inclusion is based.

32. You have been asked to serve on a districtwide committee to examine the possible overrepresentation of students from culturally and linguistically diverse backgrounds in special education programs. Identify and discuss four areas you would want the committee to examine related to this issue.

33. Discuss the outcomes and implications of the following cases:

   Brown v. Topeka Board of Education
   Hobson v. Hansen
   Diana v. California State Board of Education
   Lau v. Nichols
   Larry P. v. Riles
   Board of Education of the Hendrick Hudson School District v. Rowley
   Irving Independent School District v. Tatro
   Timothy W. v. Rochester, N.H. School District
   Agostini v. Felton

Matching Questions

Applying what you have read about the continuum of educational placements, match the educational placement to its level in the continuum of educational services available to students with disabilities. Begin with Option 1 as the most integrated setting through to Option 10 as the most highly segregated setting.

Educational Placement	Level
A. Homebound instruction	1. _____ Option 1
B. Special education classroom with part time in the general education classroom	2. _____ Option 2
C. General education classroom with collaboration teacher assistance	3. _____ Option 3
	4. _____ Option 4
D. Full-time special education classroom	5. _____ Option 5
E. General education classroom with few or no supportive services	6. _____ Option 6
	7. _____ Option 7
F. Residential schools	8. _____ Option 8
G. General education classroom with resource room assistance	9. _____ Option 9
H. Hospitals or institutions	10. _____ Option 10
I. General education classroom with itinerant specialist assistance	
J. Special day schools	

Chapter 2: Understanding the Diverse Educational Needs of Students with Disabilities

Chapter Overview

Chapter two introduces issues related to the special education identification process, and meeting the needs of students with high- and low-incidence disabilities. The chapter presents concepts such as the prereferral and placement system for students with disabilities, the Individualized Education Program, and the various special education categories. The chapter begins with a case study about *Marty,* a student with varied educational needs. This case provides a framework for discussing factors that educators should consider in designing an appropriate education for students, like *Marty*, who have diverse educational needs.

Chapter Objectives

Upon completion of this chapter, students should be able to:

1. Understand how the special education identification process works.
2. Identify the components of an individualized education program (IEP) and how to implement IEPs in general education settings.
3. Outline the definitions of and characteristics associated with students with high-incidence and low-incidence disabilities.
4. Identify the educational needs of students with high-incidence and low-incidence disabilities.

Chapter Outline

I. *Marty* (Chapter-opening vignette)
II. How Does the Special Education Identification Process Work?
    1. Comprehensive Planning Team
    2. Prereferral System
    3. Individualized Education Program (IEP)
       a. IEP Components
       b. Special Considerations in Developing IEPs
          i. Assistive Technology
          ii. Transition Services
       c. Student Involvement
       d. Implementing IEPs in General Education Settings
III. What Are the Educational Needs of Students with High-Incidence Disabilities?

Chapter Summary

Chapter two has provided information on the educational needs of students with disabilities and how their needs can be met in inclusive classrooms. The chapter contained information on the special education identification process, which includes the planning team, the prereferral and referral systems, the individualized education program, and the special education categories. Information on students with high-incidence disabilities, including students with learning disabilities, mild emotional and behavioral disorders, speech or language impairments, and attention deficit disorders, was presented in chapter two. In addition, the chapter contained information on students with low-incidence disabilities, which includes students with physical, sensory, and multiple disabilities.

Key Terms

Comprehensive planning team   Prereferral system   Diabetes

Individualized education program   Transition services   Autism

Learning disability   Emotional and behavioral disorders   Asthma

Traumatic brain injury   Seizure Disorder

Attention deficit disorders   Mental retardation

Speech and language disorders   Orthopedically impaired

Hearing impairments   Cerebral palsy

Other health impaired   Visual impairments

Spina bifida (Myelomeningocele)   Tourette syndrome

Hyperglycemia   Hypoglycemia

Learning Activities

1. Assume you are the general education teacher of a student who is experiencing difficulty keeping pace with the general education curriculum. You have sought the help of a teacher assistance team to gather information about your student, and to help you develop and implement new methods in an effort to keep your student in the general education classroom. As a member of the teacher assistance team, collaborate with other team members to write a script of the team meeting, which you will role-play in class. Explain why you have selected these methods.

2. A second language learner has been referred to the comprehensive planning team for possible placement in a special education class. Working as a member of a small group, identify how you would differentiate whether the student's behavior is a result of a learning/language disorder or a cross cultural/linguistic difference. As group members, present and explain your responses to the class.

3. Working in a cooperative group, use assessment data regarding a student to create an IEP based on this assessment information. Be sure to pay attention to various aspects of IEP development as presented in the chapter including IEP components, special considerations in developing IEPs, student involvement, and implementing IEPs in

general education settings.

4. List the characteristics of students with learning disabilities on transparencies. Repeat this procedure for students with emotional and behavioral disorders, students with attention deficit disorders, students with mental retardation, and students with speech and language disorders. Develop reasons for the increase in the number of students identified as learning disabled. Develop and list plausible reasons for the increase in the number of students identified as learning disabled. Show the transparencies, discuss the similarities and differences among classifications, review the definitions of each disability category, and share the reasons why your group thinks that students with learning disabilities are being increasingly identified.

5. Using the web and the library, conduct research on methods that have been found to be effective in working with students with physical and health needs, sensory, and multiple disabilities. Evaluate these methods and prioritize them in terms of your perception of their effectiveness for use with these students. Share your findings with your classmates.

6. Research various organizations and support services that are available for students with low-incidence disabilities in your local community. Select a student with a low-incidence disability and develop a portfolio of the services that are available for him or her in your community. Share your findings with the class and with an educator who teaches students with high-incidence disabilities.

7. Select and research one of the high- or low-incidence disabilities presented in this chapter. Use the information to develop a brochure on this disability, which you will share with the class. Discuss with the class how you would support and help students with this disability in the classroom.

8. Conduct a library search for adolescent or children's literature books on one of the disabilities you read about in this chapter. Make a list of the books, along with a brief description of each, which you will share with the class.

Guided Review

Marty

1. Read the vignette *Marty* and answer the following questions.

a. What difficulties was *Marty* experiencing in class?

_____

_____

b. What steps did Ms. Tupper, *Marty's* teacher, take to help him?

_____

_____

_____

_____

c. What did the members of the school district's Comprehensive Planning Team do in their efforts to help *Marty*?

_____

_____

_____

_____

d. What did the Comprehensive Planning Team members conclude?

After reading this chapter, you should be able to answer these as well as the following questions.

a. How does the special education identification process work?
b. What are the educational needs of students with high-incidence disabilities?
c. What are the educational needs of students with low-incidence disabilities?

How Does the Special Education Identification Process Work?
Comprehensive Planning Team

2. Who are the members of the Comprehensive Planning Team, and what role does each member play on the team?

Team Members of the Comprehensive Planning Team	Expertise

Prereferral System

3. Discuss the importance of prereferral strategies in addressing the needs of students from diverse backgrounds.

   a. _____

   b. _____

   c. _____

   d. _____

   e. _____

4. Define the following:

   a. Comprehensive Planning Team:

   _____

   _____

   b. Prereferral system:

   _____

   _____

Individualized Education Program (IEP)

5. What is an IEP?

   _____

6. List the seven components of IEPs as presented in your textbook.

a. _____

b. _____

c. _____

d. _____

e. _____

f. _____

g. _____

Special Considerations in Developing IEPs

7. In addition to the components of the IEP, the IEP team must also consider special factors related to the unique needs of students. What are these special factors?

_____

_____

_____

_____

_____

_____

8. In making the determination regarding whether a student requires assistive technology, the IEP team must make a determination based on an individualized technology evaluation. What does this evaluation include?

a. _____
b. _____
c. _____
d. _____
e. _____

9. What areas might the transition services component of the IEP address?

a. _____
b. _____
c. _____

What Are the Educational Needs of Students with High-Incidence Disabilities?

10. List the disability categories that are referred to as high-incidence or mild disabilities.

a.

b.

c.

d.

11. What percentage of students with disabilities comprises students with high-incidence disabilities?

_____

Students with Learning Disabilities

12. What is a learning disability?

_____

_____

_____

13. The textbook describes three categories of learning disabilities. Describe characteristics of students in each of the categories.

Category of Learning Disability	Characteristics
Learning Difficulties	
Language and Communication Difficulties	
Perceptual and Motor Difficulties	

Social-Emotional and Behavioral Difficulties	

Students with Emotional and Behavioral Disorders

14. How does the IDEA define emotional disturbance?

_____

_____

_____

15. According to the IDEA, what five characteristics should be exhibited for a student to be classified as emotionally disturbed?

a. _____

_____

b. _____

_____

c. _____

_____

d. _____

_____

e. _____

_____

16. Identify three characteristics of students who are mildly emotionally disturbed?

a.

b.

c.

17. As educators, you should be aware that students with emotional and behavioral disorders might be particularly vulnerable to depression and suicide. What are some warning signs of depression and suicide that you should be aware of?

a.

b.

c.

d.

18. What are some strategies that you can use to help a student who is threatening suicide?

a.

b.

c.

d.

e.

Students with Attention Deficit Disorders

19. According to the American Psychiatric Association, what is attention deficit disorder?

20. What are the three subtypes of ADD?

a.   b.   c.

21. List the characteristics of the three subtypes of ADD.

Subtype of ADD	Characteristics
Students with AD/HD	
Students with ADD/WO	
Students with AD/HD-C	

22. Students with ADD can become eligible to receive services under what laws?

a. _____

b. _____

23. What are some strategies that may be used in teaching students with ADD?

a. _____

b. _____

c. _____

d. _____

e. _____

Students with Mental Retardation

24. Write out the IDEA's definition of students with mental retardation?

_____

_____

_____

25. What are the main characteristics of students with mental retardation?

_____

_____

_____

26. Complete the following table to demonstrate the IDEA's classification system of students with mental retardation.

IDEA Classification	IQ Range
a.	
b.	
c.	

Students with Speech and Language Disorders

27. According to the IDEA, what is a speech/language impairment?

_____

_____

_____

28. What are some environmental factors that may result in communication disorders.

a. _____

b. _____

c. _____

d. _____

e. _____

29. What is receptive language?

_____

_____

30. What is expressive language?

_____

_____

31. According to your textbook, expressive language problems may be due to speech disorders that include articulation disorders. Using the following table, give examples of articulation disorders and cite an example of each.

Articulation Disorder	Example
a.	
b.	
c.	
d.	

What Are the Educational Needs of Students with Low-Incidence Disabilities?

32. Which groups of students are referred to as students with low-incidence disabilities?

a.

b.

c.

33. What percentage of the students with disabilities comprises students with low-incidence disabilities?

_____

Students with Physical and Health Needs

34. What two types of students with physical and health needs that are recognized by the IDEA, how are these students defined, and what impairments or students are included in these types?

Types of Students	Definition	Types of Impairments or Students

Students with Cerebral Palsy

35. Match the primary type of cerebral palsy with its description.

Type of Cerebral Palsy	Description
a.	Difficulties in balancing and using the hand
b.	Jerky, exaggerated, and poorly coordinated movements
c.	Uncontrolled and irregular movements
d.	Loose, flaccid musculature

36. What causes cerebral palsy?

_____

Students with Spina Bifida

37. What is another name for spina bifida? _____

38. What is a cause of spina bifida?

_____

39. What are some of the needs of students with spina bifida?

a.
b.
c.

40. How can you help the school nurse to meet the needs of students with spina bifida?

a. _____
b. _____
c. _____
d. _____
e. _____

Students with Asthma

41. What is asthma?

_____

_____

42. What are some of the symptoms of asthma?

a.   b.   c.   d.   e.

43. What are some conditions that trigger an asthma attack?

a.   b.   c.   d.   e.

44. What are some children's literature books that you can use to teach students about asthma and allergies?

a.

b.

c.

d.

Students with Tourette Syndrome

45. What is Tourette syndrome?

_____

46. What are symptoms of Tourette syndrome?

a.   b.   c.   d.

e.   f.   g.   h.

Students with Diabetes

47. What are symptoms of diabetes that you as a teacher need to know?

_____
_____
_____

48. Hyperglycemia and hypoglycemia are two serious medical conditions that can occur in the classroom. What are these conditions? Describe symptoms of these conditions.

Name of Condition	Description	Symptoms
Hyperglycemia		
Hypoglycemia		

49. Describe how a teacher may help students with diabetes succeed in school.

_____
_____
_____

_____
_____
_____
_____

Students with Seizure Disorders

50. Fill in the information about the types of seizures.

Type of Seizure	Characteristics
Tonic-Clonic	
Tonic Seizure	
Absence Seizure	
Complex Partial Seizure	

Students Treated for Cancer

51. What can you as a teacher do to help students with cancer and their peers deal with concerns they may have about this disease?

_____
_____
_____
_____

Medically Fragile Students

52. How does the Council for Exceptional Children's task Force on Medically Fragile Students define medically fragile students?

53. Medically fragile students have a variety of chronic and progressive conditions. List some of these conditions.

a.   b.   c.

54. How can you help medically fragile students succeed in school?

_____

_____

_____

_____

_____

Students with Traumatic Brain Injury

55. How does the IDEA define traumatic brain injury?

_____

_____

_____

56. Describe how students with traumatic brain injury differ from students with learning and behavioral problems.

_____

_____

_____

57. How can you help students with TBI in the classroom?

_____

_____

_____

_____

Students with Autism

58. What is autism and when does it usually occur?

_____

_____

_____

59. What are characteristics of autism?

a.   b.   c.

60. What is Asperger's syndrome?

_____

61. What are some characteristics of students with Asperger's syndrome?

a.   b.   c.

62. What are some teaching and classroom management strategies that teachers can use in working with students with autism?

_____

_____

_____

_____

Students with Severe and Multiple Disabilities

63. What types of disabilities are included under the category severe and multiple disabilities?

_____

_____

64. Describe characteristics of students with severe and multiple disabilities.

a. _____

b. _____

c. _____

d. _____

65. What can you do to help students with severe and multiple disabilities succeed in the inclusive classroom?

a. _____

b. _____

c. _____

d. _____

e. _____

f. _____

g. _____

h. _____

Medication Monitoring

66. Name some of the students who may be taking prescription drugs.

a.   b.   c.

Students with Sensory Disabilities

67. Which two groups of students are regarded as students with hearing impairment?

a.   b.

Students with Hearing Impairments

68. How does the IDEA define students who are deaf?

_____

_____

_____

_____

69. How does the IDEA define the term hard of hearing?

_____

_____

_____

70. What does the audiometric test measure?

_____

_____

_____

71. Depending on the hearing levels, the student with a hearing impairment may use the following methods to communicate. Describe the characteristics of each method presented in the following table.

Method	Characteristics
Oral/Aural	
Manual	
Bilingual-Bicultural	
Total Communication	

72. How does the deaf culture movement view individuals with hearing impairments?

_____

_____

Students with Visual Impairments

73. How does the IDEA define visual disability?

_____

_____

74. Describe characteristics of the following classifications of students with visual impairments.

Classification	Characteristics
Low Vision	
Functionally Blind	
Totally Blind	

75. How can you help a student with a visual impairment improve his or her educational performance in school?

Application Exercise for Chapter 2

Read "What Would You Do in Today's Diverse Classroom" and answer the following questions based on the vignette.

a. What prereferral strategies might be appropriate for Samuel, Ethel, Tony, and Sadie?

b. Do you think that these students qualify for special education services? If so, under which disability category do they qualify? If not, why not?

c. What goals should their IEPs address, and what services should they receive to meet those goals?

d. How would placement in a general education classroom benefit these students?

e. As their teacher, what concerns would you have about having Samuel, Ethel, Tony, and Sadie in your class?

f. What resources would be helpful to you in meeting their educational needs?

Reflective Exercises for Chapter Two

1. It has been noted that over 80% of the nation's students could be identified as having learning disability using the current definition of the term learning disabilities. How many of the students you work with could qualify using this definition? What is it about the definition that allows so many students to be identified as having a learning disability?

2. What are your views regarding the need for and effectiveness of medications for students?

For Your Information

1. Whitten and Dieker (1995) offer guidelines for employing prereferral interventions in schools, and Baca and de Valenzuela (1998) and Ortiz and Wilkinson (1991) describe effective prereferral models for use with students from culturally and linguistically diverse backgrounds.

2. Campbell, Campbell, and Brady (1998), and Roberts and Baumberger (1999) offer guidelines for selecting goals and objectives for IEPs; and Etscheidt and Bartlett (1999) present a model for determining supplementary aids and services for students' IEPs.

3. Galvin and Scherer (1996) offer guidelines on evaluating and selecting appropriate assistive technology devices and involving individuals with disabilities in the selection process.

4. *The Self-Directed IEP* (Martin, Marshall, Maxson, & Jerman, 1996a, 1996b) includes lesson plans, student workbook assignments, vocabulary, discussions of expected behaviors, a teacher's manual, and videos to teach students to be actively involved in the IEP process.

5. Stough and Baker (1999) provide information that can assist you in identifying and treating depression in students.

6. Anderegg and Vergason (1992) outline the legal decisions that have defined a teacher's responsibilities when dealing with suicidal students, and Poland (1995) offers policies that schools should establish regarding suicide.

7. ADD is often diagnosed in students with learning disabilities, emotional disturbance, and reading problems (Forness, Keogh, Macmillan, Kavale, & Gresham, 1998; Riccio & Jemison, 1998).

8. DuPaul and Eckert (1998) review the academic interventions for students with ADD; and Kemp, Fister, and McLaughlin (1995) offer strategies for teaching academic skills to students with ADD, including materials to guide teaching.

9. Wadsworth and Knight (1999) developed the Classroom Ecological Preparation Inventory (CEPI) to help comprehensive planning teams collect information to place students with physical and health needs in general education classrooms.

10. Best, Bigge, and Sirvis (1994) offer guidelines for adapting classroom materials and writing utensils to students with physical disabilities.

11. Rowley-Kelley and Reigel (1993) offer guidelines for preventing skin breakdown in students who use wheelchairs, including making sure that students are positioned properly and moved periodically so that they shift their body weight; giving students opportunities to leave their wheelchairs and use prone standers, braces, and crutches; and examining students' skin for redness and swelling.

12. Getch & Neuharth-Pritchett (1999), Hill (1999), and McLoughlin and Nall (1995) offer guidelines and strategies that can be used when working with students who have asthma and allergies.

13. Michael (1995) and Spiegel, Cutler, and Yetter (1996) offer guidelines for working with students with seizure disorders.

14. Peckham (1993) developed a sample lesson plan and guidelines for teaching students about cancer that can be adapted for other chronic and serious conditions.

15. Hill (1999) offers sample forms that school districts can use to identify and plan for students special physical and health care needs, including student information checklists, individualized health care, transportation, treatment and emergency care plans, activity participation forms, communication logs, and entry/reentry checklists.

16. Stuart and Goodsitt (1996), Doelling and Bryde (1995), Phelps (1995), and Clark (1996) offer guidelines for helping students who have been hospitalized make the transition to school.

17. Marks et al. (1999) provides guidelines for educating students with Asperger's syndrome in inclusive classrooms.

18. Giangreco, Cloninger, and Iverson (1998) have developed *Choosing Options and*

48

Accommodations for Children (C.O.A.C.H.). It offers assessment, a curriculum, and teaching and communication strategies for use with students with severe disabilities in inclusive settings.

19. Engelman, Griffin, Griffin, and Maddox (1999) and Haring and Romer (1995) provide guidelines for helping students who are deaf-blind in inclusion classrooms.

20. An estimated 2 to 3 percent of all students and 15 to 20 percent of students receiving special education are taking medications to treat learning and behavioral disorders (Sweeney, Forness, Kavale, & Levitt, 1997).

21. Pancheri and Prater (1999), Sweeney et al., (1997), and Schulz and Edwards (1997) provide overviews and summaries of the potentially positive effects and negative side effects of the most commonly prescribed drugs for students.

22. Sources of Braille Reading Materials, a list of organizations that offer Braille reading materials, is available from the National Library Service for the Blind and Physically Handicapped (**www.loc.gov/nls.Braille**, 202-707-9275).

SELF-TEST FOR CHAPTER 2

Directions: Select the best answer for each question. Try to answer each question, even though you might be unsure of the best answer. Remember that this is a practice test. You will not be penalized for guessing. However, before you take your class examinations, you should clarify with the instructor whether you will be penalized for guessing.

Multiple Choice Questions

1. A system whereby a team of educators works collaboratively to provide assistance to classroom teachers prior to considering a student for a special education placement is referred to as:
   a. MAPS.
   b. Circle of friends.
   c. A priori.
   d. Prereferral .

2. Which statement about individualized education programs (IEPs) is **true**?
   a. IEPs must include a statement of the needed transition services for students beginning no later than age 16
   b. IEPs should include a determination of whether a student with a disability requires assistive technology devices or services
   c. IEPs should include a description of the related services students will need to benefit from special education
   d. All of the above

3. Students with learning disabilities may have:
   a. Memory and attention problems.
   b. Social and behavioral problems.
   c. Language problems.
   d. All of the above

4. Which statement is **false** concerning students with emotional and behavioral disorders?
   a. These students are underidentified
   b. The intellectual abilities of these students vary
   c. These students rarely have learning problems
   d. These students have high rates of inappropriate behavior

5. Students with attention deficit disorders who are not associated with overactivity are referred to as:
   a. Students without hyperactivity.
   b. Attention deficit disorder combined.
   c. Attention deficit disorder with hypoactivity.
   d. Differentiated attention deficit disorder.

6. Students with mild mental retardation have IQ scores that range from:
   a. 10 to 20.
   b. 50 to 75.
   c. 30 to 50.
   d. 20 to 30.

7. The major cause of mild mental retardation is:
   a. Genetic and chromosomal disorders.
   b. Social-environmental factors.
   c. Infectious diseases.
   d. Gestational and obstetric disorders.

8. Receptive language refers to:
   a. The manner in which an individual expresses words and sentences.
   b. The ability to understand spoken language.
   c. The quality of the sounds produced.
   d. None of the above

9. A student often omits sounds in words. For example, the student says "og" instead of "dog." The student may have:
   a. An articulation disorder.
   b. A receptive language disorder.
   c. A voice disorder.
   d. A fluency disorder.

10. An individual with cerebral palsy whose movements are jerky, exaggerated, and poorly coordinated has what type of cerebral palsy?
    a. Hypotonia
    b. Athetosis
    c. Hypertonia
    d. Ataxia

11. This is the most common childhood chronic illness and the leading cause of absence from school:
    a. AIDS
    b. Traumatic Brain Injuries
    c. Juvenile Arthritis
    d. Asthma

12. A student exhibits involuntary tics and uncontrolled laughing that occurs and disappears at various times. This student may have:
    a. Cerebral palsy.
    b. Mental retardation.
    c. Tourette syndrome.
    d. Spina bifida.

13. Administering an audiometric test assesses the degree of hearing loss. The frequency of sound is measured in:
    a. db.
    b. Hz.
    c. Pd.
    d. None of the above

14. Braille can promote effective reading and writing if used by students who are:
    a. Slightly blind.
    b. Functionally blind.
    c. Low in vision.
    d. Low in albumin.

True or False Questions

Directions: Read each statement carefully. Circle true if the answer is true, and false if the answer is false.

15. Students with mild disabilities make up the largest percentage of students with disabilities.
    True   False

16. According to the federal government, 15% of the students in our nation's schools have learning disabilities.
    True   False

17. Students with mild emotional and behavior disorders may resemble students with learning disabilities and mild mental retardation.
    True   False

18. Expressive language refers to the ability to understand spoken language.
    True   False

19. There has been a dramatic increase in the number of students with mild retardation and a significant decrease in the number of students with learning disabilities.
    True   False

20. Research indicates that the performance of students with learning disabilities is similar to their peers.
    True   False

21. The majority of cases of mental retardation are caused by biomedical factors.
    True   False

22. As a group, students with physical and health conditions tend to have IQ scores within the normal range.
    True   False

23. Children with hyperglycemia are sometimes thirsty, tired and lethargic, and have breath that has a sweet, fruity odor.
    True   False

24. Students who are medically fragile may not need special education.
    True   False

Sentence Completion Questions

25. IEPs for students who are 14 years or older must include an annual statement of the _____ services that will help these students.

26. _____ is a type of cerebral palsy where the individual experiences difficulties in balancing and using hands.

27. The intensity of a sound that an individual can hear is defined in terms of _____, while the frequency of a sound is measured in _____.

28. _____ language refers to the ability to understand spoken language.

29. _____ is a condition that is caused by a defect in the vertebrae of the spinal cord.

Essay Questions

30. What is a prereferral system?

31. Describe five strategies for assisting students with attention deficit disorders.

32. Discuss strategies that teachers can use to help students with speech and language disorders.

33. What are the symptoms of diabetes? How would you respond if a student went into diabetic shock?

Matching Questions

Match the strategies for accommodating students with traumatic brain injury (TBI) with the effects of TBI.

Strategies for Accommodating Students with TBI	Effects of TBI
1. ____ Check comprehension regularly	A. Cognitive and Academic Skill Impacts
2. ____ Provide opportunities to practice transition routines	B. Language Impacts
3. ____ Provide strategies and skills for dealing with anger and frustration	C. Social Impacts
4. ____ Use survey and preview techniques	D. Organizational Skill Impacts
5. ____ Provide opportunities for structured and unstructured communication exchange	
6. ____ Provide diagrams, maps, charts, or other graphic cues	
7. ____ Implement schedule systems	
8. ____ Target behaviors of greatest concern and implement behavioral change gradually	

Chapter 3: Understanding the Diverse Educational Needs of Learners Who Challenge Schools

Chapter Overview

Chapter three continues the discussion of the concept of inclusion and the challenges of its implementation. Specifically, chapter three discusses societal changes, their impact on students and schools, and explains alternative philosophies for structuring schools to address these changes. Some of the issues discussed in this chapter include economic changes, demographic shifts, discrimination and bias, and family changes, and their effects on students and schools; addressing the needs of students from culturally and linguistically diverse backgrounds; differentiating cultural and language differences from learning problems; and addressing the educational needs of students who are gifted and talented.

Chapter Objectives

Upon completion of this chapter, students should be able to:

1. Discuss how schools need to change to address the societal shifts that have resulted in a growing number of students whose needs are challenging the educational system.
2. Outline alternative philosophies for structuring schools to address societal changes.

Chapter Outline

I. *Carol* (Chapter-opening vignette)
II. How Have Economic Changes Affected Students and Schools?
    1.   A Nation of Rich and Poor
    2.   Poverty
    3.   Urban Poverty
        a. Homelessness
    4.   Rural Poverty
        a. Children of Migrant Workers
        b. Native Americans
    5.   Suburban Poverty
        a. Wealthy Children
III. How Have Demographic Shifts Affected Students and Schools?
    1.   Immigration
    2.   Students Who Are Immigrants

Chapter Summary

Chapter three presented information on how societal changes have helped to make inclusive education necessary to meet the needs of an increasing culturally and linguistically diverse group of students who challenge the existing school structure. The following issues were discussed in chapter three: economic changes, demographic shifts, discrimination and bias, and family changes, and their effects on students and schools; addressing the needs of students from culturally and linguistically diverse backgrounds; differentiating cultural and language differences from learning problems; and addressing the educational needs of students who are gifted and talented.

Key Terms

Poverty	Homelessness	Migrant Students
Cornucopia kids	Demographic shifts	Immigration
Bilingual education	Second language acquisition	Multiple intelligences
Racial discrimination	Gender bias	Gay and lesbian youth
HIV/AIDS	Family changes	Child abuse
Substance abuse	Multicultural education	

Learning Activities

1. Interview professionals with expertise and experience in providing services to the poor and homeless about their work.

2. Visit bilingual education programs and English as a Second Language Programs. Keep a journal of your observations.

3. Observe classrooms and interview a diverse group of students concerning their experiences in schools. Present your observations to the class in such a way that it requires group discussion.

4. Conduct further research and prepare a class presentation on the experiences of multiracial children in schools, and strategies for working with multiracial children. See if you can interview someone who is multiracial about his or her experiences in school and society. Share your findings with the class.

5. Read a book written about migrant children and their families. Write a book report and/or describe how you would use this book in a classroom to develop sensitivity and respect for migrant children and their families.

6. Interview educators in local schools about the numbers and types of students who receive services for gifted and talented students. Ask them to discuss the procedures used to identify these students and how these students are educated. Chart and compare the numbers of students receiving services by ethnicity. Research why some ethnic groups are underrepresented and others overrepresented in programs for gifted and talented students. Discuss your findings with the class.

7. Research information about students with HIV/AIDS. Prepare a brochure that defines HIV/AIDS, outlines how the disease is contracted, delineates universal precautions for teachers and students, and enumerates available treatment options.

8. Plan and present a skit about child abuse, gay and lesbian youth, or substance abuse. After presenting the skit, lead a discussion on the key issues raised.

9. Write a poem about affluent or poor and homeless children. Share your poem with students in your class.

Guided Review

Carol

1. Read the vignette *Carol* and answer these questions.

a. What factors led to some of the difficulties that Carol had in school?

b. Should Carol have been placed in a special education class?

c. How does inclusion affect students like Carol?

After reading this chapter, you should be able to answer these as well as the following questions.

a. How have economic changes affected students and schools?
b. How have demographic shifts affected students and schools?
c. What are the needs of students from culturally and linguistically diverse backgrounds?
d. How can I differentiate cultural and language differences from learning problems?
e. What are the educational needs of students who are gifted and talented?
f. What is the impact of discrimination and bias on students and schools?
g. How have family changes affected students and schools?
h. What are some alternative philosophies for structuring schools to address societal changes?

How Have Economic Changes Affected Students and Schools

2. The textbook reported that Brantlinger (1995) interviewed poor and affluent students to identify and understand their perspectives on the impact of socioeconomic status on schooling. What were five of her findings?

a. _____

b. _____

c. _____

d. _____

3. What are four of the effects of poverty on children?

a. _____

b. _____

c. _____

d. _____

4. What is the Stewart B. McKinney Homeless Assistance Act?

_____

_____

_____

5. List five major barriers that prevent many homeless students from attending school?

a. _____
b. _____
c. _____
d. _____
e. _____

6. How can you assist homeless and economically poor students?

a. _____
b. _____
c. _____
d. _____
e. _____

7. Outline three factors that are associated with the migrant lifestyle.

a. _____

b. _____

c. _____

8. How can teachers improve the school adjustment and performance of migrant students?

_____

_____

_____

_____

_____

9. How many Native Americans live in remote rural areas?

_____

10. What term does Baldwin (1989) use to describe affluent children?

_____

11. Describe some of the characteristics of affluent children?

_____

_____

_____

_____

How Have Demographic Shifts Affected Students and Schools?

12. What is the rate of population growth in the United States since 1980?

_____

13. What do the population projections suggest about school-age children of color?

_____

_____

_____

14. Describe the stages that many immigrants go through as they struggle to adjust to a new country.

_____

_____

_____

_____

15. Discuss some of the problems that students who are immigrants are likely to encounter.

_____
_____
_____
_____
_____
_____

16. List five ways you can facilitate the education of students who are immigrants.

a. _____
b. _____
c. _____
d. _____
e. _____

17. Explain the Supreme Court decision in *Plyler v. Doe*.

_____
_____
_____
_____

18. Explain the following:

a. Bilingual Education
b. Bilingual Education Act
c. Two-Way Bilingual Education Program
d. English as a Second Language

What Are the Needs of Students from Culturally and Linguistically Diverse Backgrounds?

19. Describe stage-setting behaviors of some African American students?

_____
_____
_____
_____

20. Explain how the following cultural factors may affect performance in schools.

a. Time

b. Movement

How Can I Try to Differentiate Cultural and Language Differences from Learning Problems?

21. What are basic interpersonal communication skills (BICS), cognitive/academic language proficiency (CALP), silent period, language proficiency, language dominance, language preference, and code switching?

Basic Interpersonal Communication Skills (BICS)

Cognitive/Academic Language Proficiency (CALP)

Language Proficiency

Language Dominance

Language Preference

Code Switching

What Are the Educational Needs of Students Who Are Gifted and Talented?

22. How does the Gifted and Talented Children's Act of 1978 define gifted and talented children?

_____
_____
_____

23. List and describe Gardner's (1993) eight areas in which individuals may exhibit their intelligence and talent.

a. _____
   _____

b. _____
   _____

c. _____

d.

_____

e. _____

f. _____

g. _____

h. _____

24. List four ways in which you can adapt your teaching program for gifted and talented students.

a. _____

b. _____

c. _____

d. _____

What Is the Impact of Discrimination and Bias on Students and Schools?

25. Summarize the findings of educators who have explored the differential treatment of female and male students in schools.

_____

_____

_____

_____

_____

26. What are five strategies that you could consider to create an inclusive and supportive classroom for gay and lesbian youth and youth who are questioning and exploring their sexual identity?

a. _____

b. _____

c. _____

d. _____

e.

_____

_____

27. Explain the difference between HIV and AIDS.

_____

_____

_____

_____

28. What was the Supreme Court ruling in *School Board of Nassau County, Florida et al. v. Arline?*

_____

_____

_____

_____

29. Describe some strategies that a teacher could use to create an inclusive and supportive classroom for students with AIDS.

_____

_____

_____

How Have Family Changes Affected Students and Schools?

30. Discuss the following types of families.

Single-Parent Families

Extended Families

Families Headed by Gay and Lesbian Parents

Foster Families

31. Describe five strategies that you can use to create an inclusive and supportive classroom for students whose families are undergoing changes.

a. _____

b. _____

c. _____

d. _____

e. _____

32. Describe physical and behavioral indicators associated with child abuse.

_____
_____
_____
_____
_____
_____
_____

33. Describe five of the signs that indicate possible substance abuse.

a. _____
b. _____
c. _____
d. _____
e. _____

34. Describe five characteristics of substance-abused newborns.

a. _____
b. _____
c. _____
d. _____
e. _____

What Are Some Alternative Philosophies for Structuring Schools to Address Societal Changes?

35. Discuss ways in which philosophies such as inclusion and multicultural education pose challenges to schools to meet the needs of all students?

_____
_____
_____

36. What is multicultural education?

_____

_____

_____

37. Discuss similarities between multicultural education and inclusion.

_____

_____

_____

_____

_____

_____

_____

Application Exercise for Chapter 3

Read "What Would You Do in Today's Diverse Classroom" and answer the following questions.

a. How would placement in a general education class benefit Carl, Erica, Zoltan, and Julia?

b. What concerns would you have about having these students in your class?

c. What are the educational needs of Carl, Erica, Zoltan, and Julia? What would be your goals for them?

d. What strategies could you use to address their educational needs?

e. What resources would be helpful to you in meeting their educational needs?

Reflective Exercises for Chapter 3

1. Teaching in a rural area presents many unique professional and personal challenges. Could you teach and live in a rural setting? Why or Why not?

2. Rosibel and her family arrived in the United States several months ago. After Rosibel applied for free lunch, the principal asked you to obtain Rosibel's Social Security number. As Rosibel's teacher, what would you do? (Developed by Elizabeth Sealey)

3. If you moved to another country that had a different language and culture when you were in fourth grade, what aspects of school would be difficult for you? Would you

want to receive your academic instruction in English or the language of your new country?

4. How has your cultural background affected your learning style? Your teaching communication styles?

5. Because of the failure of mainstream schools to educate African American students effectively, several urban school districts have proposed separate schools for African American boys. Do you think this separation by gender and race is appropriate?

6. A disproportionate number of male students are placed in special education classes. Is this an example of discrimination in schools?

7. Kevin, a student in your class, has been misbehaving and failing to complete his homework. Your principal tells you to talk to his family. You are concerned about their reaction, as they frequently use physical punishment to discipline Kevin. What would you do? What professionals might assist you?

8. We refer to students who have needs that challenge the school system as *at risk, handicapped, culturally disadvantaged,* or *linguistically limited.* How might things be different if we referred to schools as *risky, disabling, disadvantaging,* and *limiting?*

For Your Information

1. A national migrant hotline (800-234-8848) is available to provide migrant families access education, health, housing, and other supportive services.

2. Garcia and Malkin (1993) offer educators a variety of strategies for enhancing intercultural understanding.

3. Hertzog (1998a) outlines the roles of gifted education specialists in creating inclusive gifted education programs that address the needs of ALL students, and Sternberg (1996) offers strategies to promote creativity in the classroom.

4. Kerwin and Ponterotto (1994) offer a list of resources for multiracial students and their families and educators, including support groups, correspondence clubs, publications, recommended readings, and books.

5. Set Your Sites: You can obtain additional information and resources about these eating disorders from the National Eating Disorders Organization (www.laureate.com/nedointro.html 800-322-5173), as well as from the National Association of Anorexia Nervosa and Associated Disorders at its Web address (www.member.aol.com/anadzo/index.html 847- 831-3438).

6. Lipkin (1992) has developed a high school curriculum offering teachers and counselors guidelines, strategies, and resources for designing and implementing classroom lessons on gay, lesbian, and bisexual issues.

7. Stroud, Stroud, and Staley (1997) offer guidelines for working with adoptive parents and their children as well as a list of children's books about adoption.

8. Bryde (1998), and McCarty and Chalmers (1997) have compiled a list of children's literature on differences in family structures.

9. Bryde (1998) has compiled a list of children's books that deal with child abuse

SELF-TEST FOR CHAPTER 3

Direction: Select the best answer for each question.

Multiple Choice Questions

1. These factors may result in difficulties in school for students who are not disabled:
   a. Demographic shifts
   b. Racism and sexism
   c. Changes in family structure
   d. All of the above

2. This group is the fastest growing poverty group in the US:
   a. Children
   b. Senior citizens
   c. Single mothers
   d. Incarcerated youth

3. Who is more likely to be harmed by poverty?
   a. Children who attend suburban schools
   b. Children who attend rural schools
   c. Children who experience poverty earlier in their lives
   d. Children who experience poverty later in their lives

4. These are strategies that have been developed by some school districts for educating homeless children:
   a. Transportation
   b. Tutoring
   c. After-school and full-year programs
   d. All of the above

5. These are concerns that have been identified by educators in rural areas:
   a. Teacher recruitment and retention
   b. Limited opportunities for inservice and preservice training
   c. Limited course offerings
   d. All of the above

6. Which of these are immigrants likely to encounter:
   a. Racism, violence, harassment
   b. Guilt, as a result of their survival
   c. Coping with sociocultural and peer expectations
   d. All of the above

7. In *Plyler v. Doe*, the Supreme Court:
    a. Ruled that all undocumented students have the same rights as US citizens to attend public schools
    b. Ruled that the practice of tracking was unconstitutional
    c. Ruled that Special Education classes were discriminatory and segregated students
    d. Established procedures for nondiscriminatory testing

8. Second language acquisition involves two distinct types of skills:
    a. DIBS and CAL
    b. CIBS and CALS
    c. BICS and CALP
    d. None of the above

9. The degree of skill exhibited in speaking a language is:
    a. Language dominance
    b. Language proficiency
    c. Code switching
    d. Language preference

10. These can provide data on a student's language performance:
    a. Standardized tests
    b. Observations and language samples
    c. Questionnaires and interviews
    d. All of the above

11. In the *Board of Nassau County, Florida et al. v. Arline*, the Supreme Court ruled that individuals with infectious diseases are covered under:
    a. The Rehabilitation Act
    b. The Americans with Disabilities Act
    c. The Individuals with Disabilities Education Act
    d. None of the above

12. An estimated 6 to 14 million children live in families headed by:
    a. Grandparents
    b. Parents
    c. Mothers
    d. Gay and lesbian

13. Substance abuse is more widespread among:
    a. Suburban and rural students
    b. Urban and suburban students
    c. Rural and urban students
    d. None of the above

True or False Questions

Directions: Read each statement carefully. Circle true if the answer is true, and false if the answer is false.

14. Nearly 20 percent of US children live in poverty.
    True   False

15. The Stewart B. McKinney Homeless Assistance Act guarantees homeless children the right to a free appropriate education in a mainstreamed school environment.
    True   False

16. Bilingual education does **not** employ the native and the new language and culture of students to teach them.
    True   False

17. A student cannot be found to have a disability due to language disabilities.
    True   False

18. Substance abuse rates are roughly equal for boys and girls.
    True   False

Sentence Completion Questions

19. A basic component of _____ programs is instruction in English as a second language.

20. Poverty is prevalent in American cities, where about _____ percent of all students live in poverty.

21. One group of culturally and linguistically diverse students who live in rural areas are the children of _____.

22. Even though we often think that the _____ are affluent, many poor people also live there.

23. One integrated example of a bilingual education program is a _____ program that mixes students who speak languages other than English with students who speak English.

Essay Questions

24. Discuss how the following societal changes have contributed to the movement toward inclusion and multicultural education.

    Demographic Shifts   Immigration

    Family Changes   Poverty

25. Discuss how urban and rural poverty can affect the social and academic development of students.

26. Discuss the educational needs of students who are gifted and talented, and provide examples of strategies you would use to meet the educational needs of these students.

27. You suspect a student is a victim of child abuse. Outline the steps you would take in reporting this situation.

Matching Question

Gardner uses the framework of multiple intelligences to outline at least eight areas in which individuals may exhibit their intelligence and talent. Match the areas of intelligence and talent with their descriptions.

Descriptions	Areas of Intelligence and Talent
1. ____ Sensitivity to the sounds and functions of language	A. Verbal-linguistic
2. ____ Ability to understand the environment	B. Logical-mathematical
3. ____ Ability to understand one's strengths and weaknesses	C. Visual spatial
4. ____ Ability to deal with the abstract	D. Musical
5. ____ Ability to understand and respond to the feelings, moods, and behaviors of others	E. Bodily kinesthetic
6. ____ Ability to make something or participate in a production	F. Interpersonal
7. ____ Ability to appreciate a sense of rhythm, pitch, and melody	G. Intrapersonal
8. ____ Ability to create and interpret visual experiences	H. Naturalistic

Chapter 4: Creating Collaborative Relationships and Fostering Communication

Chapter Overview

Chapter four provides strategies for creating an inclusive environment that supports learning for all students. This chapter introduces the members of the comprehensive planning team and provides strategies for establishing collaborative relationships and fostering communication with professionals and family members.

Chapter Objectives

Upon completion of this chapter, students should be able to:

1. Understand the roles, responsibilities, and perspectives of the different members of the planning team and communication network.
2. Identify the factors that contribute to the development of a successful interactive and collaborative communication network.
3. Facilitate communication and collaboration among educators.
4. Promote congruence regarding students' educational programs.
5. Foster communication and collaboration with families.
6. Understand and address the diverse needs and experiences of families.
7. Use community resources to address the needs of students and their families.

Chapter Outline

I. *The Smith Family* (Chapter-opening vignette)
II. Who Are the Members of the Comprehensive Planning Team?
   a. Family Members
   b. School Administrators
   c. General Educators
   d. Special Educators
   e. Paraeducators and Volunteers
   f. School Psychologists
   g. Speech and Language Clinicians
   h. Social Workers
   i. School Counselors
   j. Vocational Educators
   k. School Physicians and Nurses

l. Physical and Occupational Therapists

m. Staff from Community Agencies

    n. Professionals for Students Who Are Second Language Learners

    o. ESL Teachers

    p. Bilingual Educators

    q. Migrant Educators

III. How Can Members of the Comprehensive Planning Team Work Collaboratively?

1. Employ Collaborative and Interactive Teaming

2. Use the Map Action Planning System

3. Work in Cooperative Teaching Arrangements

4. Employ Collaborative Consultation

5. Promote Congruence

    a. Meetings

    b. Student Interviews

    c. Notecard Systems

    d. Online Services

IV. How Can I Foster Communication and Collaboration with Families?

1. Gain the Trust of Families

2. Ensure Confidentiality

3. Meet Regularly with Families

    a. Plan the Meeting

    b. Structure the Environment to Promote Communication

    c. Conduct the Conference

    d. Teleconferencing

4. Address the Diverse Needs, Backgrounds, and Experiences of Families

    a. Cultural Factors

    b. Linguistic Factors

    c. Socioeconomic Factors

    d. Use Written Communication

        i. Informative Notice

        ii. Newsletters

        iii. Daily Note

        iv. Two-Way Notebooks

        v. Daily Report Cards

        vi. Home-School Contracts

    e. Employ Technology-Based Communications

    f. Encourage Family Observations

    g. Offer Training to Families

        i. Who Should Receive Training?

        ii. What Is the Content of the Training Program

        iii. Where Will Training Occur?

        iv. How Do You Train Families?

Chapter Summary

Chapter four presented guidelines for establishing an inclusive learning environment that supports the learning of all students by creating collaborative relationships and fostering communication among professionals, families, and community members. The chapter presented information on the members of the comprehensive planning team, how the members of the team can work collaboratively, and how team members can foster communication and collaboration with families.

Key Terms

Comprehensive planning team   Paraeducators   Confidentiality

Collaborative and interactive teams   Collaborative consultation   Congruence

Learning Activities

1. Interview individuals who have served on comprehensive planning teams. Ask them to discuss the discipline and perspective they represent, the types of services they provide, the roles they perform on the team, how the comprehensive planning team works, and the actions the team takes.

2. Observe a comprehensive team meeting. Since the information discussed at the meeting will be confidential, you must obtain permission to attend the meeting. Additionally, you should not share any personally identifying information.

3. Observe a bilingual educator, English as a Second Language (ESL) teacher, migrant educator, and a speech/language clinician in their classrooms.

4. Role play a comprehensive planning team meeting with other members of your class.

5. Work with other students in your class to develop a network of communication for a student with: (a) learning disabilities; (b) mental retardation; (c) behavior disorders; (d) speech and language impairments; (d) a physical and health related disability; (e) a hearing impairment; (f) a visual impairment; and (g) a student who is a second language learner. The elements of the network should contain: (a) the purpose of the network; (b) the agencies and individuals involved; (c) the services each member of the network will provide; and (d) the procedures for maintaining the network. Ask each group to share its product with the class.

6. Interview professionals and parents who have been involved with successful interactive teams about their experiences with interactive teaming.

7. Role play, with other members of your class, the steps involved in implementing the Map Action Planning System.

8. Interview educators who are involved in cooperative teaching and collaborative consultation to speak to the class about their experiences.

9. Work in cooperative groups to develop a system for a school that promotes congruence. Share your product with the class.

10. Interview parents of students with diverse needs about their experiences. Parents can discuss: (a) their reactions and their child's reactions to their child's educational placement; (b) the roles they perform in their child's education; (c) their experiences with due process; (d) their training needs and the training they have received; (e) their experiences with and reactions to parent-professional conferences; (f) the communication systems they have used with schools; and (g) any cultural, linguistic, and socioeconomic factors that served as barriers to their child's education.

11. Design, role play, and videotape a parent conference. Discuss the videotaped conference with your classmates.

12. Develop a list of available community resources for individuals with disabilities. Information concerning each agency on the list can be presented on a file card and shared with other members of the class.

Guided Review

The Smith Family

1. Read the vignette *The Smith Family* and answer the following questions:

a. What factors made this meeting successful?

b. What strategies could professionals and families employ to help students such as Paul learn better?

After reading this chapter, you should be able to answer these as well as the following questions.

a. Who are the members of the comprehensive planning team?
b. How can members of the comprehensive planning team work collaboratively?

Who Are the Members of the Comprehensive Planning Team?

2. What is the purpose of the comprehensive planning team?

_____

_____

_____

_____

_____

3. What are the roles of the following members of the comprehensive planning team?

General Educators:

Special Educators:

Paraeducators and Volunteers:

School Psychologists:

Speech and Language Clinicians:

Social Workers:

School Counselors:

Vocational Educators:

School Physicians and Nurses:

Physical and Occupational Therapists:

Staff from Community Agencies:

Professionals for Students Who Are Second Language Learners:

English as a Second Language Teachers:

Migrant Educators:

How Can Members of the Comprehensive Planning Team Work Collaboratively?

4. Discuss the following characteristics of successful collaborative and interactive teams.

   a. Legitimacy and autonomy:

   b. Purposes and objectives:

   c. Competencies of team members and clarity of their roles:

   d. Role release and role transitions:

   e. Awareness of the individuality of others:

   f. Process of team building:

   g. Attention to factors that impact on team functioning:

   h. Leadership styles:

   i. Implementation procedures:

   j. Commitment to common goals:

5. Discuss the following interpersonal roles that members of interactive teams can perform to facilitate the team's ability to function efficiently and establish a positive, trusting working environment:

   a. Initiating:

   b. Information gathering and sharing:

   c. Clarifying and elaborating:

   d. Summarizing:

   e. Consensus building:

   f. Encouraging:

   g. Harmonizing and compromising:

   h. Reflecting:

i. Balancing:

6. Describe the Map Action Planning System.

7. In MAPS, team members, including students with disabilities, their families, and peers, meet to develop an inclusion plan by initially responding to certain questions. What are these questions?

a. _____
b. _____
c. _____
d. _____
e. _____
f. _____
g. _____
h. _____

8. What are cooperative teaching teams?

_____
_____
_____
_____
_____

9. Describe some of problems that members of a cooperative teaching team may encounter.

a. _____
b. _____
c. _____
d. _____
e. _____

10. How can participants ensure that each member of the cooperative teaching team performs relevant and meaningful roles?

a. _____
b. _____
c. _____
d. _____
e. _____
f. _____
g. _____
h. _____

11. What is collaborative consultation?

_____
_____
_____
_____

12. Describe the steps in collaborative consultation.

a. _____
_____

b. _____
_____

c. _____
_____

d. _____
_____

13. What are three barriers to consultation?

a. _____
b. _____
c. _____

14. An important component of working collaboratively is the need to promote congruence. What is congruence?

_____
_____
_____

15. Describe the following remedial instruction models:

a priori model:

post hoc model:

16. Discuss four ways to foster congruence.

a. _____
_____

b. _____
_____

c.

_____

d. _____

_____

How Can I Foster Communication and Collaboration with Families?

17. List and discuss five ways to foster communication and collaboration with families.

a. _____

_____

b. _____

_____

c. _____

_____

d. _____

_____

e. _____

_____

18. How does a family's level of acculturation, beliefs about schooling, and prior experience with discrimination, impact the collaboration and communication process?

_____

_____

_____

_____

_____

_____

Application Exercise for Chapter 4

Read "What Would You Do In Today's Diverse Classroom" and answer the following questions based on the vignette.

a. What problem(s) are you encountering in each situation?

b. What would you do to address the situation?

c. What individuals, resources, and support could assist you in addressing the situation?

Reflective Exercises for Chapter 4

1. Think about a situation in which you worked collaboratively with a team. How was the outcome affected by the collaboration? What problems did the team have in working collaboratively? How did the team resolve these problems?

2. Given families' and students' rights to confidentiality, what would you do in the following situations? (1) Teachers are discussing students and their families during lunch in the teachers' lounge. (2) You notice that the students' records in your school are kept in an unsupervised area.

3. Think about several persons you talk to regularly. How do their communication styles differ in terms of eye contact, wait time, word meanings, facial and physical gestures, voice quality, personal space, and physical contact? How do these differences affect you? How do you adjust your communication style to accommodate these differences?

4. Have you used e-mail, the Internet, or a telephone answering machine to communicate with others? What were the advantages and disadvantages? How do these systems affect the communications and the information shared? What skills do educators and family members need to use these systems effectively and efficiently?

5. Do you or someone else have a family member with a disability? What has been the impact of this individual on other family members? What types of training would benefit the family?

For Your Information

1. Fradd (1993) offers guidelines for creating teams and communication networks to meet the needs of students from culturally and linguistically diverse backgrounds.

2. Doyle (1997) provides guidelines, resources, and activities that you and your paraeducators can use to work collaboratively in inclusive settings.

3. Salend, Dorney, & Mazo (1997) describe the roles of bilingual special educators in creating inclusive classrooms.

4. Williams and Fox (1996) offer a model that comprehensive planning teams can use to foster inclusion of students.

5. Davern, Ford, Marusa, and Schnorr (1993) offer a framework that you can use to evaluate teams working in inclusive settings.

6. Vargo (1998) and Kirschbaum and Flanders (1995) provide questions and forms, respectively, that allow educators to plan teaching adaptations. This is done by sharing information on topics to be covered, dates on which topics and lessons will be taught, and potential teaching adaptations.

7. Dennis and Giangreco (1996) offer suggestions for interacting with families in culturally sensitive ways.

8. Locust (1994) offers information about the cultural beliefs and traditional behaviors of Native Americans that may affect the teaching of Native American students with disabilities.

9. Many school districts are establishing multilingual hot lines to communicate school-related information to families in their native languages.

10. Boone, Wolfe and Schaufler (1999) provide guidelines for preparing written communication to families.

11. Translators who help to prepare written communications and community members can help educators develop culturally relevant and sensitively written documents (Fradd & Wilen, 1990).

12. Cramer et al. (1997) and Meyer and Vadasy (1994) provide guidelines on offering workshops and activities for siblings of children with special needs.

13. Alper, Schloss, and Schloss (1994), McDonald, Kysela, Martin, & Wheaton, (1996), and Miller and Hudson (1994) offer guidelines for improving family information sessions, using family support groups, and helping families learn to be advocates for their children, respectively.

14. Searcy, Lee-Lawson, and Trombino (1995) offer guidelines for using family members as mentors to help educate other family members.

SELF-TEST FOR CHAPTER 4

Directions: Select the best answer for each question. Try to answer each question, even though you might be unsure of the best answer. Remember that this is a practice test. You will not be penalized for guessing. However, before you take your class examinations, you should clarify with the instructor whether you will be penalized for guessing.

Multiple Choice Questions

1. Which of the following describe(s) the comprehensive planning team?
   a. Provides appropriate services to students and their families
   b. Solves problems and coordinates services available to students
   c. Team members vary depending on students', families', and educators' needs
   d. All of the above

2. When these persons work too closely with students with disabilities, they can impede effective inclusion programs.
   a. General education teachers
   b. Special education teachers
   c. Paraeducators
   d. Bilingual educators

3. They can help rule out or confirm a language disability:
   a. Speech and language clinician
   b. Special educators
   c. General educators
   d. None of the above

4. She/He serves as a liaison between the home and the school and community agencies:
   a. Vocational educator
   b. School nurse
   c. School physician
   d. Social worker

5. They help students adapt to impaired or lost motor function:
   a. Community workers
   b. Social workers
   c. Physical and occupational therapists
   d. Vocational educators

6. Bilingual educators:
   a. Teach curriculum areas using two languages
   b. Assess and teach students
   c. Help students maintain their native culture
   d. All of the above

7. A systems approach to designing a plan for students is:
   a. FAST Planning System
   b. Map Action Planning System
   c. Finding Out Planning System
   d. Circle Planning System

8. Cooperative teaching:
   a. Minimizes some problems of pull-out programs
   b. Allows supportive services
   c. Modifies teaching for students with academic difficulties without labeling them
   d. All of the above

9. A teaching arrangement whereby general and special educators work together in one classroom and have responsibility and accountability for all instructional activities is:
   a. Interactive teaching
   b. Incidental teaching
   c. Cooperative teaching
   d. Shared teaching

10. In the "post hoc" model for promoting congruence:
    a. Supportive instruction reinforces skills previously introduced in the general education classroom.
    b. The supportive services educator reviews and reteaches content previously covered in the general education classroom.
    c. a and b
    d. None of the above

11. Factors for involving and empowering families include:
    a. Level of acculturation
    b. Beliefs about schooling
    c. Prior experience with discrimination
    d. All of the above

True or False Questions

Directions: Read each statement carefully. Circle true if the answer is true, and false if the answer is false.

12. The general educator assists the special educator with teaching modifications.
    True   False

13. Nurses, not physicians, provide many medically related services.
    True   False

14. When a migrant family moves into a new area, it is certified as being eligible for migrant status and services.
    True   False

15. Legitimacy and autonomy are **not** characteristics of effective collaborative and interactive teams.
    True   False

16. Teachers involved in cooperative teaching remove students from the general education classroom for supportive services.
    True   False

17. Cooperative teaching teams encounter minimal to no problems.
    True   False

18. Evaluation is **not** a step in collaborative consultation.
    True   False

19. Family involvement and empowerment are based largely on the trust established between families and educators.
    True   False

20. One way of fostering communication with families is by improving the quality of family-teacher conferences.
    True   False

21. Schools are mandated to offer training to families so that they will be able to perform various roles in the educational process.
    True   False

Sentence Completion Questions

22. The _____ makes collaborative decisions about the educational needs of students.

23. A _____ who supervises the district-wide services usually serves as the chairperson of the comprehensive planning team.

24. _____ can aid the team by performing diagnostic tests to assess the students' physical development, sensory abilities, medical problems, and central nervous system functioning.

25. _____ are interested in their child's education, but different cultural perspectives often make it hard to establish traditional school-family interactions.

26. The extent to which members of one culture adapt to a new culture is referred to as _____.

Essay Questions

27. Identify and briefly discuss 6 dimensions of successful interactive teams.

28. Identify and discuss 5 effective interpersonal and communication skills that interactive team members can perform to facilitate the team's ability to function efficiently and establish a positive, trusting environment.

29. What is the Map Action Planning System (MAPS)? List the questions that the mainstreaming network should address when using the MAPS.

30. Describe cooperative teaching arrangements.

Matching Question

Match the method that the comprehensive planning team members use to collaborate with the description.

Description	Method
1. ____ Based on common assessment results, goals and objectives, teaching strategies, and materials	A. Interactive team
2. ____ A systematic approach for designing a plan for students	B. Map Action Planning System
3. ____ General education teachers and other supportive personnel collaborate to teach students in inclusive settings.	C. Cooperative teaching
4. ____ Team members have legitimacy and autonomy	D. Collaborative consultation
5. ____ Professionals work collaboratively with the general education teacher who has primary responsibility.	E. Congruent program

Chapter 5: Creating an Environment the Fosters Acceptance and Friendship

Chapter Overview

Chapter five provides strategies for creating an inclusive environment that supports learning for all students. The chapter presents strategies that support learning by fostering acceptance of individual differences related to disability, culture, language, gender, and socioeconomic status, and promoting friendships among students.

Chapter Objectives

Upon completion of this chapter, students should be able to:

1. Discuss the role students can perform to facilitate the success of inclusion and mainstreaming.
2. Outline the factors that contribute to the development of attitudes toward students with individual differences.
3. Use a variety of strategies to assess attitudes toward students with individual differences.
4. Use a variety of strategies to teach students acceptance of individual differences related to disability.
5. Use a variety of strategies to teach students acceptance of individual differences related to culture, language, gender, and socioeconomic status.
6. Use a variety of strategies to facilitate the development of friendships.

Chapter Outline

I.   *Mr. Monroig* (Chapter-opening vignette)
II.   How Do Attitudes Toward Individual Differences Develop?
III.   How Can I Assess Attitudes Toward Individual Differences?
    a. Attitude Assessment Instruments
    b. Knowledge of Individual Differences Probes
    c. Students' Drawings
IV.   How Can I Teach Acceptance of Individual Differences Related to Disability?
    a. Attitude Change and Information-Sharing Strategies
    b. Teacher Attitudes and Behaviors
    c. Disability Simulations
    d. Successful Individuals with Disabilities
    e. Guest Speakers
    f. Films and Books

Chapter Summary

This chapter offered a variety of strategies for teaching students to accept individual differences and facilitate friendships. As you review this chapter, consider the following questions and try to remember the points to answer the questions: (a) How do attitudes toward individual differences develop? (b) How can I assess attitudes toward individual differences? (c) How can I teach acceptance of individual differences related to disability? (d) How can I teach acceptance of individual differences related to culture, language, gender, and socioeconomic status? (e) How can I facilitate friendships?

Key Terms

Sociograms   Probes   Equal-status relationship

Disability simulations	Adaptive devices	Cultural diversity
Language diversity	Dialect differences	Sociolinguistic education
Gender equity	Family differences	Homelessness
Migrant lifestyle	stereotyping	Discrimination

Learning Activities

1. Work with three classmates to review books, television shows, commercials, cartoons, stories in newspapers, and movies that examine how individuals with disabilities, women, and individuals from diverse cultural and linguistic backgrounds are portrayed. Ask each group to present and explain their findings.

2. Use observations, sociograms, attitude change assessment instruments, knowledge of individual differences probes, and students' drawings to assess the attitudes of students toward individuals with disabilities. Share your findings with the class.

3. Demonstrate the steps for conducting and interpreting the findings of a sociogram by doing a class sociogram.

4. Select a book about individuals with disabilities and evaluate the book by addressing the guidelines presented in this chapter. Additionally, each group should role play how they would use the book with a group of students. Their role play should include use of discussions, simulations, explanations and other activities to highlight information to be learned about individuals with disabilities.

Guided Review

1. Read the vignette *Mr. Monroig* and answer the following question.

a. What other strategies can Mr. Monroig use to help his students understand and accept individual differences and develop friendships?

After reading this chapter, you should be able to answer this as well as the following questions.

a. How do attitudes toward individual differences develop?
b. How can I assess attitudes toward individual differences?
c. How can I teach acceptance of individual differences related to disability?
d. How can I teach acceptance of individual differences related to culture, language, gender, and socioeconomic status?
e. How can I facilitate friendships?

What Factors Contribute to the Development of Attitudes Toward Individual Differences?

2. Research indicates that by the age of___, students are cognizant of and curious about cultural and physical differences.

3. Summarize the findings of research studies regarding how students view their peers with disabilities.

_____

_____

_____

_____

_____

4. List and discuss two factors that contribute to the development of negative attitudes toward students with individual differences.

a. _____

_____

_____

b. _____

_____

_____

How Can I Assess Attitudes Toward Individual Differences?

5. Describe the following techniques/instruments for assessing students' knowledge and acceptance of individual differences.

Assessment Instrument	Description
1. Acceptance Scale	
2. Personal Attribute Inventory for Children	
3. Individual Differences Probes	
4. Student Drawings	

How Can I Teach Acceptance of Individual Differences Related to Disability?

6. What does *equal status relationship* mean?

_____

_____

_____

7. Explain how the following can be used to facilitate acceptance of individual differences

Examine teacher attitudes and behaviors:

Disability simulations:

Lessons and assignments on successful individuals with disabilities:

Guest speakers:

Films and books:

Instructional materials:

Information about adaptive devices:

Collaborative problem solving:

How Can I Teach Acceptance of Individual Differences Related to Culture, Language, Gender, and Socioeconomic Status?

8. This section presents several ways to teach acceptance of individual differences. Discuss two ways to foster acceptance of individual differences related to culture.

_____

_____

_____

_____

9. Discuss how educators can teach about linguistic diversity.

_____

_____

_____

_____

_____

10. What is African-American English?

_____
_____
_____
_____

11. What are some phonological features of African-American English?

_____
_____
_____
_____
_____

12. What are some syntactical features of African-American English?

_____
_____
_____
_____
_____

13. What are some stylistic elements of African-American English?

_____
_____
_____
_____
_____

14. Give three examples of rhetorical elements of African-American English?

a. _____
_____
b. _____
_____
c. _____
_____

15. Explain the bridge system.

_____
_____
_____
_____
_____

16. Define sociolinguistic education and discuss how it can be used to foster an understanding and appreciation of linguistic diversity.

_____
_____
_____
_____
_____

17. How can you help students to understand the importance of gender equity?

_____
_____
_____
_____
_____

18. How can students be taught about homelessness and the migrant lifestyle?

_____
_____
_____
_____
_____

19. What are five strategies that teachers can implement to overcome negative attitudes and misconceptions about AIDS?

a. _____

b. _____

c. _____

d. _____

e. _____

20. Discuss several strategies that teachers can use to help students respond to stereotyping and discrimination.

_____
_____
_____
_____
_____

How Can I Facilitate Friendships?

21. Discuss five ways that you could facilitate the development of friendships.

a. _____
_____

b. _____
_____

c. _____
_____

d. _____
_____

e. _____
_____

Application Exercise for Chapter 5

Read "What Would You Do in Today's Diverse Classroom?" and answer the following questions.

a. What are some of the factors that might result in your students having difficulties socializing with one another?
b. What are some other ways you could identify your students' attitudes toward each other?
c. What are some strategies you could implement to encourage your students to accept each other's individual differences?
d. What are some strategies you could use to facilitate the development of friendships among your students?

Reflective Exercises for Chapter 5

1. When you were growing up, did you have opportunities to interact with children and adults with disabilities? How did these experiences help you understand and accept individual differences?

2. How are individuals with disabilities and those from various cultural and linguistic backgrounds pictured in books, television shows, movies, and cartoons? How do these portrayals affect you and your students= understanding and acceptance of individual differences?

3. What are your attitudes and behaviors in regard to individual differences? Are there

individual differences with which you feel very comfortable? Uncomfortable? How do you reveal these attitudes to others? How did you develop these attitudes and behaviors?

4. Simulate several disabilities for part or all of a day. How did the simulations make you feel? How did others treat you? What problems did you experience? What did you learn? How did you adapt to the various disabilities?

5. Think about how to use collaborative problem solving in the following situation. In social studies class, students are required to take notes. Some of the students have trouble doing this. What solutions do you think other students would suggest?

6. Think about a situation in which you were stereotyped. What factors contributed to that stereotype? How did it make you feel? How did it affect the outcome of the situation? Think about a situation in which you stereotyped someone. What factors contributed to your holding that stereotype? How did it make you feel? What would you do differently?

7. Think about how you would respond to the following situations: Students are telling anti-Semitic jokes; using terms such as *Indian giver;* mimicking a student's accent; denying their racial, ethnic, or religious identities; teasing a male student who likes to sew.

8. Make a circle of friends for yourself. How have your friends and support group assisted you during stressful times?

For Your Information

1. Additional simulation activities are available in Freedman-Harvey and Johnson (1998), Hallenback and McMaster (1991), Horne (1998), Raschke and Dedrick (1986), and Wesson and Mandell (1989).

2. Safran (1998, 2000) offers a list of films about individuals with disabilities and guidelines for selecting and using them in classrooms.

3. Smead (1999) offers an annotated bibliography of 24 books presenting personal accounts of exceptionality.

4. Menkart (1999) offers guidelines on enhancing the effectiveness of heritage month celebrations.

5. Reviews and lists of children's literature about various cultures and religions across a wide range of grade levels are available (Book Links Advisory Board, 1994; Consortium of Latin American Studies Programs, 1998; Kaplan, 1994; Kea, 1998;

Mandlebaum et al., 1995; Miller-Lachman & Taylor, 1995; Office of Diversity Concerns, 1999; Taylor, 2000). You also can obtain additional information on multicultural children's literature by contacting the Council on Interracial Books for Children (212-757-5339).

6. Tiedt and Tiedt (1995) describe a variety of activities that teachers can use to help students learn about and value linguistic diversity.

7. Day (1998) has developed a program to teach standard American English to African-American English speakers.

8. Odean (1997) provides an annotated bibliography of over 600 books about girls.

9. Banks (1991a) and Tiedt and Tiedt (1995) identify many resources and activities for teaching students about discrimination.

10. Aronson (1997) provides resources for teaching your students about individual differences related to body size and type.

11. DeGeorge (1998) compiled a list of children's books about friendship and described a model for using children's literature to teach friendship skills.

12. Rosenthal-Malek (1997) has developed a metacognitive strategy social skills training program to help students develop their friendship-making skills.

13. Fad, Ross, and Boston (1995) offer guidelines for using cooperative groups to promote friendships and teach social skills.

14. Hughes et al. (1999) describe the steps in creating a high school peer buddy system.

15. Salend and Schobel (1981) developed a positive approach to name-calling, which involves implementing a series of activities to teach students the importance, meaning, derivation, and function of names, as well as the negative effects of calling others names.

16. Falvey, Coots, and Terry-Gage (1992) offer lists of extracurricular activities for preschool, elementary, and secondary students.

SELF-TEST FOR CHAPTER 5

Directions: Select the best answer for each question. Try to answer each question, even though you might be unsure of the best answer. Remember that this is a practice test. You will not be penalized for guessing. However, before you take your class examinations, you should clarify with the instructor whether you will be penalized for guessing.

Multiple Choice Questions

1. You can change negative attitudes toward individuals perceived as different by using:
   a. Stereotypic Scales
   b. Social helping aids
   c. Attitude change and information-sharing strategies
   d. None of the above

2. Which does **not** promote acceptance of language diversity?
   a. Using diverse cultural referents
   b. Teaching students native languages
   c. Using peers to tutor students in their native language
   d. Maintaining books on monocultural perspectives

3. Grammatical and stylistic differences between African-American English and standard English can be attributed to differences between African languages and:
   a. English
   b. Spanish
   c. Portuguese
   d. French

4. Gender equity activities help to combat:
   a. Equality
   b. Sexism
   c. Acceptance
   d. All of the above

5. Teachers can create a friendly environment by using:
   a. Cooperative grouping
   b. Technology-based collaborative activities
   c. Activities that promote class cohesiveness
   d. All of the above

6. Research on attitudes toward individual differences suggest that:
   a. Students with learning disabilities are more accepted than students with physical disabilities.
   b. Males with learning problems are more likely to be rejected than females with learning problems.
   c. Younger students possess less favorable attitudes than older students.
   d. Young children are aware of and curious about physical differences.

7. Which is a goal of attitude change and information-sharing strategies?
   a. To establish an equal-status relationship
   b. To provide information and direct contact with others
   c. To provide information to counter stereotyped views
   d. All of the above

8. Teachers can model appropriate language by using speech that:
   a. Sets students apart
   b. Describes students by their disabilities
   c. Describes students by their abilities
   d. Respects students' feelings

9. When teaching students about family differences, teachers should:
   a. First accept their own families
   b. Acknowledge various family arrangements of students
   c. Select projects at random
   d. Assume that students live in traditional families

10. When teaching students about cultural diversity, teachers should:
    a. Focus the discussion on a limited number of cultures
    b. Focus the program on celebrations of holidays of different cultures
    c. Help students see the similarities among groups through their differences
    d. All of the above

True or False Questions

Directions: Read each statement carefully. Circle true if the answer is true and false, if the answer is false.

11. By the age of 1, students are aware and curious about cultural and physical differences.
    True   False

12. Students without disabilities do **not** have negative attitudes toward their peers.
    True   False

13. Peers view poor students with disabilities more positively than wealthy students.
    True   False

14. Research suggests that most students hold favorable attitudes toward their peers with disabilities.
    True   False

15. Exposure to books about individuals with disabilities alone is a highly effective attitude change strategy.
    True   False

16. Individual differences probes are used to assess students' knowledge about various groups.
    True   False

17. Disability simulations are effective in teaching students about individual differences.
    True   False

18. Books and videos are **not** effective in teaching students about individual differences.
    True   False

19. Commercial materials can be used to teach students about individual differences.
    True   False

20. Collaborative problem solving does not sensitize students regarding problems they might encounter in the general education classroom.
    True   False

Sentence Completion Questions

21. Observations and _____ may be used to assess students' social interactions.

22. Drawings of scenes depicting other individuals can be used to assess students' _____ toward others.

23. The Alexander Graham Bell Association for the Deaf provides a video that simulates different types of _____.

24. Negative perceptions of others can be referred to as _____.

25. _____ teach students who are not disabled about disabilities through experiences that resemble how it feels to be disabled.

Essay Questions

26. You are developing a unit to teach students acceptance of individual differences related to disability. As part of the unit, you intend to use disability simulations. Outline the guidelines you would follow in using disability simulations.

27. You observe students telling anti-Semitic jokes and mimicking a student's accent. How would you respond to these incidents?

28. What is sociolinguistic education? How can educators use sociolinguistic education to promote an acceptance of linguistic diversity?

29. You notice that several students are isolated during social times and appear to have no friends. Identify and discuss five ways you could help facilitate friendships among students.

Matching Question

Match the following terms with the correct descriptions.

Descriptions	Terms
1. ____ Ability to speak Portuguese and English	A. Equal status relationship
2. ____ Can be integrated in multiple aspects of the curriculum	B. Simulations
3. ____ Saying an African American boy likes to work in cooperative groups when he likes to work independently	C. Bilingualism
4. ____ Role play responds to friendship-making situations	D. Sociolinguistic education
5. ____ Individuals view each other as equal.	E. Stereotyping
6. ____ Experiencing how it feels to have a disability	F. Social skills instruction

Chapter 6: Creating Successful Transitions to Inclusive Settings
Chapter Overview

Chapter six provides a framework for helping students make the transition to inclusive environments and from school to adulthood. It also provides strategies for helping students develop self-determination.

Chapter Objectives

Upon completion of this chapter, students should be able to:

1. Discuss the strategies for helping students make transitions to inclusive settings.
2. Teach students to use learning strategies and promote independent work skills in students.
3. Employ a variety of strategies to plan a program to help students who speak languages other than English make transitions to inclusive settings.
4. Employ a variety of strategies to promote the generalization of skills.
5. Delineate the factors that educators should consider in helping students from specialized schools and early education programs make transitions to inclusive schools within their communities.
6. Employ a variety of strategies to promote the successful transitions of students who are exiting schools.
7. Promote the development of self-determination in their students.

Chapter Outline

I. *Nick* (Chapter-opening vignette)
II. How Can I Help Students Make the Transition to General Education Classrooms?
    1. Understand Students' Unique Abilities and Needs
    2. Use Transenvironmental Programming
       a. Environmental Assessment
       b. Intervention and Preparation
          i. Teach Classroom Procedures and Successful Behaviors
          ii. Use Preteaching
          iii. Use Videos
          iv. Teach Learning Strategies
          v. Designing Learning Strategies
       c. Promote Students' Independent Work Skills
          i. Written Assignments
          ii. Independent Assignments
       d. Develop Students Organizational Skills

                    i. Assignment Notebooks
                    ii. Assignment Logs
                    iii. Daily and Weekly Schedules

3.   Generalization

II.   How Can I Help Students from Specialized Schools and Preschool Programs Make the Transition to Inclusive Settings?

1.   Plan the Transitional Program
2.   Adapt Transitional Models

III.   How Can I Help Students from Linguistically and Culturally Diverse Backgrounds Make the Transition to Inclusive Settings?

1.   Plan the Transition Program
2.   Adapt Transitional Models

IV.   How Can I Help Students from Linguistically and Culturally Diverse Backgrounds Make the Transition to Inclusive Settings?

1.   Teach Cultural Norms
2.   Orient Students to the School
3.   Teach Basic Interpersonal Communication Skills
       a. Modeling
       b. Role Playing
       c. Prompting
       d. Scripting
4.   Teach Cognitive Academic Language Proficiency Skills
       a. Cognitive Academic Language Learning Approach
       b. Content-Based Curriculum
       c. Academic Language Development
       d. Learning Strategy Instruction
5.   Offer Newcomer Programs

V.   How Can I Help Students Make the Transition from School to Adulthood?

1.   Develop an Individualized Transition Plan
2.   Prepare Students for Employment
       a. Competitive Employment
       b. Supported Employment
       c. Job Coach
3.   Career Education Programs
       a. Elementary School Years
       b. Middle School/Junior High Years
       c. High School Years
4.   Service Learning Programs
5.   Functional Curriculum and Career Education Models
6.   Foster Independent Living Arrangements
7.   Promote Student Participation in Leisure Skills
       a. Leisure Education
       b. Recreational and Leisure Resources for Individuals with Disabilities
8.   Explore Postsecondary Opportunities

VI.   How Can I Help Students Develop Self-Determination?

1. Offer Choices and Solicit Preferences
2. Develop Self-Advocacy Skills
3. Promote Self-Esteem
4. Provide Attribution Training
5. Provide Access to Positive Role Models
   a. Affinity Support Groups
   b. Mentors
6. Provide Access to Communications
7. Use Self-Determination Curricula

Summary

Chapter six provided guidelines for planning and using transitional programs to prepare students for success in inclusive classroom settings. The chapter also offers strategies for helping students make the transition from school to adulthood, and for helping students to develop self-determination.

Key Terms

Transition	Transenvironmental programming
Environmental assessment	Preteaching
Learning strategies	Generalization
Transitional models	Cultural norms
Basic interpersonal communication skills	Cognitive academic language proficiency
Cognitive academic language approach	Individualized transition plan
Competitive employment	Supported employment
Career education programs	Service learning programs
Functional curriculum	Career education models
Community-based living arrangements	Leisure education
Self-determination	Mentors

Learning Activities

1. Using the form developed by Salend and Viglianti (see text Figure 6.2), observe and compare several general and special education settings that serve students of the same age. Discuss the differences between the two types of settings with respect to instructional materials and support personnel, presentation of subject matter, learner response variables, student evaluation, classroom management, social interactions and physical design. Based on these observations, list five objectives of an orientation program for moving a student from a special to a general education setting.

2. Develop and implement a program to prepare a student for entry into a general education classroom. The program should include an assessment of the environment, a listing of the objectives of the transitional program, a description of the strategies for meeting the objectives of the program, plans for promoting generalization of skills and strategies for evaluating the effectiveness of the transitional program.

3. Discuss the following with a classmate: What learning strategies do you use? Are they successful? How did you learn these strategies? Teach your classmate how to use one of the learning strategies you have found to be successful.

4. Create a learning strategy.

5. Work with three classmates to develop a vignette that describes a student with a social skill deficit or language problem. Next, devise a modeling, coaching, role playing, prompting, and scripting strategy to address the problem. Share your examples with the class.

Guided Review

1. Read the vignette *Nick* and answer the following questions:

a. What additional factors should you consider when planning a transitional program to prepare students such as Nick for success in general education settings?

b. What additional transitions do students make?

c. How can you help students make these transitions?

After reading this chapter, you should be able to answer these as well as the following questions.

a. How can I help students make the transition to general education classrooms?

b. How can I help students from specialized schools and preschool programs make the transition to inclusive settings?

c. How can I help students from linguistically and culturally diverse backgrounds make the transition to inclusive settings?

d. How can I help students make the transition from school to adulthood?

e. How can I help students develop self-determination?

How Can I Help Students Make the Transition to General Education Classrooms?

2. What information can the special education teacher share with the general education teacher regarding the following groups of students who are making the transition from a special education classroom to a general education classroom?

a. Students with sensory disabilities:

_____
_____
_____

b. Students who are learning English as a second language:

_____
_____
_____

c. Students with special physical and health needs:

_____
_____
_____

3. Describe Anderson-Inman's four-step transenvironmental programming model.

a.

b.

c.

d.

4. What is involved in environmental assessment?

_____
_____
_____

5. Outline the steps involved in designing learning strategies.

_____

_____

_____

_____

6. What are cognitive credit cards?

_____

_____

_____

7. Describe the strategies and procedures of the intervention and preparation phase of the transenvironmental model.

Strategies and Procedures	Description
1. Teach classroom procedures and successful behaviors.	
2. Use preteaching.	
3. Use videos.	
4. Teach learning strategies.	
5. Promote students' independent work skills.	

8. "HOW" is a technique that can provide students with a structure for producing acceptable papers. Describe the technique.

   H =
   1.
   2.
   3.
   4.

   O =
   1.
   2.
   3.
   4.
   5.
   6.

   W =
   1.
   2.
   3.

9. Explain Archer's model for training students to complete independent assignments.

Step 1:

Step 2:

Step 3:

Step 4:

10. Describe three strategies that can help students become more organized.

a.

b.

c.

11. How can a teacher promote generalization?

_____

_____

_____

_____

_____

How Can I Help Students from Specialized Schools and Preschool Programs Make the Transition to Inclusive Settings?

12. What can teachers do in planning and implementing a transition program for students who are moving from special day schools and preschool programs to inclusive settings?

_____

_____

_____

_____

13. George, Valore, Quinn and Varisco (1997) and Goodman (1979) have developed models for integrating students from specialized schools into schools within their community that also can be adapted to plan transitions from preschool programs or from hospital and institutional settings to school. What is involved in the models?

a.   f.

b.   g.

c.   h.

d.   i.

e.   j.

How Can I Help Students from Linguistically and Culturally Diverse Backgrounds Make the Transition to Inclusive Settings?

14. What might a transitional program for students from linguistically and culturally diverse backgrounds include?

_____

_____

_____

15. What is pragmatics? _____

_____

16. Discuss four ways that teachers can help students learn different cultural behaviors?

a. _____

_____

b. _____

_____

c. _____

_____

d. _____

_____

17. Discuss the following strategies that teachers can use to help students develop basic interpersonal communication skills (BICS).

a. Modeling: _____

_____

_____

_____

b. Role Playing: _____

_____

_____

_____

c. Prompting: _____

_____

_____

_____

d. Scripting: _____

_____

_____

_____

18. Discuss strategies that can be used to facilitate the development of cognitive academic language proficiency skills.

_____
_____
_____
_____

19. Describe the following components of the cognitive academic language learning approach.

a. Content-Based Curriculum: _____
_____
_____
_____

b. Academic Language Development: _____
_____
_____
_____

c. Learning Strategy Instruction: _____
_____
_____
_____

20. Outline the services offered by newcomer programs.

a. _____
_____

b. _____
_____

c. _____
_____

d. _____
_____

How Can I Help Students Make the Transition from School to Adulthood?

21. What is the Individualized Transition Plan?

_____
_____
_____
_____

22. What is competitive employment?

_____
_____
_____

23. What is supported employment?

_____
_____
_____

24. What is the purpose of a job coach?

a. _____

b. _____

c. _____

d. _____

25. What should career education include?

_____
_____
_____
_____
_____
_____
_____
_____

26. What is a functional curriculum?

_____
_____
_____
_____

27. Describe the following functional curriculum and career education models.

Functional Curriculum/Career Education Models	Description
1. Life-Centered Career Education Model	
2. Domains of Adulthood Model	
3. School Based Career Education Model	

28. List the most common community-based living arrangements.

_____

_____

_____

_____

_____

How Can I Help Students Develop Self-Determination?

29. What is self-determination?

_____

_____

_____

30. How can you help students develop self-advocacy and self-esteem skills?

_____

_____

_____

_____

_____

_____

31. What does attribution training involve?

_____

_____

_____

_____

32. Who is a mentor?

_____

_____

_____

33. Describe your mentor if you have one and say how she/he has influenced you.

_____

_____

_____

_____

_____

_____

_____

_____

Application Exercise for Chapter 6

Read "What Would You Do in Today s Diverse Classroom?" and answer the following questions.

a. What additional information would you like to have about Carolina and Henry in order to plan a transitional program for them?

b. What goals would you have for the transitional program for Carolina and Henry?

c. What teaching and generalization strategies would you use to help Carolina and Henry make a successful transition to your class?

d. How could you promote Carolina's and Henry's self-determination skills?

Reflective Exercises for Chapter 6

1. Think about your transition from high school to college. What problems did you experience? How did peers help?

2. If you were going to make a video of your classroom and school, what features would you highlight?

3. What learning strategies do you use? Are they successful? How did you learn them? What other learning strategies might be helpful to you?

4. With which tasks and processes do your students have trouble? Can you develop a

learning strategy to help them?

5. How did you become interested in teaching? What career education programs helped you to make that decision? What job-related and interpersonal skills do you need to be an effective teacher? What career education experiences have helped you develop those skills? How did your cultural background and gender affect your career choice?

6. Would you describe yourself as self-determined? If so, how did you develop self-determination? If no, what factors hindered you?

7. Have you mentored others? Have you been mentored by others? Were these arrangements formal or informal? What roles did the mentor perform? What outcomes and barriers were associated with these experiences? Was it easier to be a mentor or a protege?

For Your Information

1. McKenzie and Houk (1993) and O'Shea (1994) offer guidelines for helping students make the transition to the general education classroom.

2. Welch (1994) offers guidelines for conducting an environmental assessment and an overview of commercially available environmental assessment instruments. Monda-Amaya et al. (1998), the Institute on Community Integration (n.d.), Fuchs et al. (1994), and George and Lewis (1991) have developed checklists, inventories, and interview protocols that can help you plan the transition to general education settings.

3. Lebzelter and Nowacek (1999) offer a checklist that you can use to evaluate learning strategies and assess their usefulness for individual students.

4. Meltzer, Roditi, Houser, and Perlman (1998) offer strategies that teachers and students can use to assess students' use of learning strategies. Montague (1997) offers questions that teachers can use to assess students' acquisition, use, maintenance, and generalization of learning strategies.

5. Ellis and Lenz (1996) offer guidelines and Heaton and O'Shea (1995) offer a mnemonic strategy called STRATEGY that can help you develop mnemonic learning strategies.

6. Hadden and Fowler (1997) and Drinkwater and Demchak (1995) offer guidelines, and forms for designing programs that help students and families make the transition from preschool and early childhood programs to inclusive schools.

7. Stuart and Goodsitt (1996), Doelling and Bryde (1995), and Phelps (1995) offer guidelines for helping students and their families make the transition from hospitals

and rehabilitation centers to school and home.

8. Romero and Parrino (1994) developed the *Planned Alternation of Languages (PAL)* approach to help prepare second language learners to make the transition to general education classes.

9. Bruns and Fowler (1999) offer guidelines for designing culturally sensitive transition plans.

10. Asselin, Todd-Allen, and deFur (1998) outline the roles and responsibilities of transition specialists to help students and their families make transitions.

11. Hutchins and Renzaglia (1998) developed a family vocational interview that you can use to involve families in the transition planning process.

12. Patton, de la Garza, and Harmon (1997) developed assessment and learning activities to prepare students for success in competitive and supported employment settings.

13. Beakley and Yoder (1998) offer guidelines for establishing community-based learning programs.

14. Heuttig and O Connor (1999); Johnson, Bullock and Ashton-Shaeffer (1999); Reilly, (1999); and Schelein, Ray, and Green (1997) provide a variety of leisure education materials, activities and resources; and Langmuir and Axelson (1996) offer resources for using assistive technology for recreation.

15. Hall, Kleinert, and Keams (2000) offer information about postsecondary programs for students with moderate and severe disabilities.

16. Wehmeyer (1996) developed a student self-report strategy that you can use to measure your students' self-determination.

17. Battle, Dickens-Wright, and Murphy (1999) offer guidelines to help students develop effective self-advocacy skills and learning strategies. PROACT (Ellis, 1998) and ASSERT (King, 2000) are available for the same purpose.

18. Duchardt, Deshler, and Schumaker (1995) developed a learning strategy called BELIEF and accompanying graphic devices to help students identify and change their ineffective attributions.

19. Stainback et al. (1994) offer suggestions for helping students form affinity support groups that are managed by the students themselves rather than by adults and that are inclusive rather than exclusive.

20. Campbell-Whatley (1999) and Miller (1997) offer guidelines for developing mentoring programs for students.

SELF-TEST FOR CHAPTER 6

Directions: Select the best answer for each question. Try to answer each question, even though you might be unsure of the best answer. Remember that this is a practice test. You will not be penalized for guessing. However, before you take your class examinations, you should clarify with the instructor whether you will be penalized for guessing.

Multiple Choice Questions

1. This is **not** true about transitions:
    a. Transitions are difficult
    b. Placement in inclusive settings requires many transitions
    c. In making transitions, students must adjust to different behavioral expectations
    d. All of the above

2. Environmental assessment involves:
    a. Determining components of the orientation program
    b. Recruiting students from culturally and linguistically diverse backgrounds
    c. Collecting varied assessment programs
    d. None of the above

3. To help identify the content of the transitional program, some schools include a _____ on the placement team.
    a. Psychologist
    b. Grandparent
    c. Classmate
    d. Nurse

4. Environmental assessment involves:
    a. Analyzing important features of the new learning environment
    b. Interviewing teachers and students
    c. a and b
    d. a only

5. These are strategies and procedures in the intervention and preparation phase of the transenvironmental model:
    a. Preteaching
    b. Videos
    c. Learning strategies
    d. All of the above

6. This is **not** a step in Archer's model for training students to complete independent assignments:
    a. Plan it
    b. Complete it
    c. Check it
    d. Paraphrase it

7. Basic Interpersonal Communication Skills include:
    a. Modeling
    b. Comprehending
    c. Role playing
    d. Prompting

8. This is **not** a component of the Cognitive Academic Language Learning Approach:
    a. Content-based curriculum
    b. Academic language development
    c. Intervention and preparation instruction
    d. Learning strategy instruction

9. This functional curriculum and career education model targets life-centered competencies:
    a. Life-Centered Career Education
    b. Map Action Planning System
    c. Domains of Adulthood Model
    d. None of the above

10. To prepare a student for entry into a general education classroom, students are gradually introduced to the curriculum of the general education classroom in the ESL program. This is an example of:
    a. Sheltered English
    b. Bilingual Transition Program
    c. Cognitive Academic Language Learning Approach
    d. Total Response Program

11. A system that provides individuals with ongoing assistance as they learn how to obtain, perform and hold a job, and travel to and from work is referred to as:
    a. Work enclave
    b. Competitive employment
    c. Supported employment
    d. Individual employment

12. One's ability to make choices and express their preferences is referred to as:
    a. Coaching
    b. Mentoring
    c. Self-attribution
    d. Self-determination

13. This can be used to show students the language and structure of social interactions
    a. Scripting
    b. Coaching
    c. Role playing
    d. Approximating the environment

14. A strategy whereby students are taught to use stimuli in the environment to facilitate the acquisition of new skills is:
    a. Role playing
    b. Coaching
    c. Prompting
    d. Scripting

True or False Questions

Directions: Read each statement carefully. Circle true if the answer is true, and false if the answer is false.

15. Beginnings and transitions are usually easy
    True   False

16. Anderson Inman's transenvironmental programming model has four steps.
    True   False

17. The contents and goals of the transitional program are **not** developed from an environmental assessment.
    True   False

18. A transitional program can help students learn how to keep track of the many activities that occur in the inclusive setting.
    True   False

19. You can promote generalization by training the students to perform under the conditions and expectations that they will encounter in the general education classroom.
    True   False

Sentence Completion Questions

20. Students with disabilities often need to make _____ to new environments.

21. Teaching students by allowing them to view appropriate examples of the desired behavior is called _____ .

22. Working with coworkers who are not disabled and being paid at least a minimum wage is called _____ .

23. A _____ is also called a supported employment specialist.

24. Students' self-determination and self-esteem can be fostered by _____, which involves teaching students to analyze the events and actions that lead to success and failure.

Essay Questions

25. Identify and describe the four steps in Anderson-Inman's transenvironmental programming model.

26. What is a learning strategy? Outline and briefly describe the steps in teaching students to use learning strategies.

27. What is the Cognitive Academic Language Learning Approach (CALLA)?

28. Several of your students need to develop self-determination. Discuss five ways you could help these students develop self-determination.

Matching Question

Cognitive Academic Language Learning Approach (CALLA) has three components. Match each component with its description.

Description	Component
1. _____ Students master techniques that make it easier to learn language and subject matter content.	A. Content-Based Curriculum
2. _____ Students are introduced to content in this sequence: science, math, social studies, and language arts.	B. Academic Language Development
3. _____ Students practice using English as the language of instruction while teachers support them by using concrete objects, visuals aids, and gestures.	C. Learning Strategy Instruction
4. _____ Students are gradually introduced to the curriculum of the general education classroom in the bilingual education program.	

Chapter 7: Creating a Classroom Environment That Promotes Positive Behavior

Chapter Overview

Chapter seven discusses ways in which you can plan and implement strategies to promote positive behaviors that foster learning and prevent students from harming each other. It also provides guidelines for designing your classroom to accommodate students' learning, social, and physical needs.

Chapter Objectives

Upon completion of this chapter, students should be able to:

1. Understand the legal guidelines educators and placement teams should consider when designing disciplinary actions for students with disabilities.
2. Understand and interpret behavior and communication within a social/cultural context.
3. Understand how to conduct a functional behavioral assessment.
4. Employ a variety of strategies to record student behavior.
5. Use an antecedents-behavior-consequences (ABC) analysis to plan appropriate strategies to modify classroom behavior.
6. Employ a variety of individually oriented strategies to promote appropriate classroom behavior.
7. Employ a variety of individually oriented strategies to decrease inappropriate classroom behavior.
8. Employ a variety of group-oriented behavior management strategies to promote appropriate and decrease disruptive behavior.
9. Employ a variety of classroom design modifications to accommodate students' learning, social, and physical needs.

Chapter Outline

I. *Jaime* (Chapter-opening vignette)
II. What Legal Guidelines Must I Consider When Designing Disciplinary Actions for Students with Disabilities?
III. How Can I Conduct a Functional Behavioral Assessment?
    1. Identify the Problematic Behavior
    2. Define the Behavior
    3. Use an Observational Recording System to Record the Behavior
       a. Event Recording
       b. Duration and Latency Recording

                    a. Token Economy System
20.   Behavior Reduction Interventions
        a. Use Redirection and Corrective Teaching
        b. Employ Interspersed Requests
        c. Use Positive Reductive Procedures/Differential Reinforcement Techniques
        d. Use Planned Ignoring
        e. Consider Verbal Reprimands

V.   How Can I Prevent Students from Harming Others
1.   Students Who Are Bullies
2.   Students with Aggressive and Violent Behaviors

VI.   How Can I Adapt the Classroom Design to Accommodate Students' Learning, Social, and Physical Needs?
1.   Seating Arrangements
2.   Teacher's Desk
3.   Teaching Materials
4.   Bulletin Boards and Walls
5.   Learning Centers and Specialized Areas
6.   Classroom Design Adaptations
        a. Students From Diverse Cultural and Language Backgrounds
        b. Students with Hearing Impairments
        c. Students with Visual Impairments
        d. Students with Health and Physical Disabilities
        e. Students with Behavior and Attention Disorders

Chapter Summary

Chapter seven offered guidelines for helping students learn in inclusive classrooms by promoting good behavior and modifying the classroom design for various types of students. The following questions were posed and answered in the chapter. Can you recall the information to answer the questions?

a. What Legal Guidelines Must I Consider When Designing Disciplinary Actions for Students with Disabilities?
b. How Can I Conduct a Functional Behavioral Assessment?
c. How Can I Promote Positive Classroom Behavior in Students?
d. How Can I Prevent Students from Harming Others
e. How Can I Adapt the Classroom Design to Accommodate Students' Learning, Social, and Physical Needs?

Key Terms

Permitted disciplinary procedures	Controlled disciplinary procedures
Prohibited disciplinary procedures	*Cole v. Greenfield-Central Community Schools*
Manifestation determination	Functional behavioral assessment
Target behavior	Event recording
Duration and latency recording	Interval recording or time sampling
Anecdotal records	Antecedents-behavior-consequences analysis
Sociocultural factors	Behavioral intervention plan
Affective education techniques	Values clarification
Life space interviewing	Teacher effectiveness training
Peer mediation	Consequence-based interventions
Group-oriented management systems	Independent group systems
Behavior reduction interventions	Positive reduction procedures/Differential reinforcement techniques

Learning Activities

1. Interview several general and special education teachers to determine the social skills and academic performance competencies that the teachers feel are important for students to be successful in the general education classroom. Discuss and analyze the responses by listing the social and academic competencies, comparing the responses of general education and special education teachers, comparing the responses of elementary, junior high and high school teachers, comparing the responses of teachers who teach different content areas, and comparing the responses of teachers from different school districts.

2. Work with three classmates to operationally define terms that are commonly used to describe student behavior such as: out of seat, noisy, aggressive, unmotivated, and

withdrawn.

3. Visit a classroom, define a behavior, and record it using the different recording systems presented in the chapter. An attempt should be made to write an anecdotal record of a student's behavior. Discuss with your classmates the problems you encountered in using each system and note the differences among the systems.

4. Discuss the rules you would institute in your classrooms. Evaluate the rules with respect to the following: (a) Is the rule necessary to prevent harm to others or their property? (b) Does the rule promote the personal comfort of others? (c) Does the rule facilitate learning? (d) Does the rule encourage the development of friendships in the classroom? (e) Does the rule prevent disrespectful behavior directed at peers, the teacher, the teacher's aide, or others in school? (f) Is the rule logical and reasonable? (g) How will the rule affect the class? and (h) Is the rule consistent with the schoolwide rules and procedures students are expected to follow?

5. Working in a cooperative learning group, prepare a schedule for a hypothetical class. Additionally, outline a plan to help students make the transitions from one period or activity to the next. Share your products with the class.

6. Design and administer a reinforcement survey.

7. Design a contingency contract.

8. Observe several individuals with whom you interact regularly. Identify the nonverbal communication strategies these individuals use when interacting with others. Discuss your findings with respect to the following: (a) What nonverbal strategies did the individuals employ? and (b) Were these nonverbal behaviors congruent with the individuals' verbal statements?

9. Work with three classmates to design an inclusive general education classroom including plans for seating arrangements, the teacher's desk, instructional materials, bulletin boards and walls, specialized areas, learning centers, and study carrels. The design also should detail specific classroom design adaptations for students from culturally and linguistically diverse backgrounds, students with hearing impairments, students with visual impairments, students with physical disabilities, students with seizures, and students with behavior and attention disorders.

Guided Review

1. Read the vignette *Jaime* and answer the following question:

a. What strategies could Ms. McLeod use to help Jaime improve his learning and behavior?

After reading this chapter, you should be able to answer this as well as the following questions.

a. What legal guidelines must I consider when designing disciplinary actions for students with disabilities?
b. How can I conduct a functional behavioral assessment?
c. How can I promote positive classroom behavior in students?
d. How can I prevent students from harming others?
e. How can I adapt the classroom design to accommodate students' learning, social, and physical needs?

2. List three essential components of an effective classroom management system.

a. _____

_____

b. _____

_____

c. _____

_____

What Legal Guidelines Must I Consider When Designing Disciplinary Actions for Students with Disabilities?

3. Explain the concept of *reasonableness.*

_____

_____

_____

4. What was the federal court's ruling in *Cole* v. *Greenfield-Central Community Schools?*

_____

_____

_____

_____

_____

_____

5. Yell and Peterson (1995) delineated three categories of disciplinary procedures used with students with disabilities. Using the following table, describe each category.

Disciplinary Procedures	Description
1. Permitted Disciplinary Procedures	
2. Controlled Disciplinary Procedures	
3. Prohibited Disciplinary Procedures	

6. Summarize the IDEA amendments of 1997 that you will have to consider when disciplining students with disabilities.

_____
_____
_____
_____
_____
_____
_____

7. What is a *manifestation determination*?

_____
_____
_____

How Can I Conduct a Functional Behavioral Assessment?

8. What is a functional behavioral assessment?

_____
_____
_____

9. Match the observational recording system with its description.

Observational Recording System	Description
A. Event Recording	1. ____ The observer records the length of time a behavior lasts.
B. Duration Recording	2. ____ Can be presented as the total length of time or as an average.
C. Latency Recording	3. ____ The observation period is divided into equal intervals and a recording of whether the behavior occurred during each interval is made.
D. Time Sampling	
	4. ____ A narrative of the events that took place during an observation.
E. Anecdotal Record	5. ____ The observer counts the number of behaviors that occurred during the observation period.
	6. ____ Latency recording is used to determine the delay between receiving instructions and beginning a task.
	7. ____ Can be summarized as the percentage of time in which a student engaged in a behavior.
	8. ____ Data are recorded as a frequency or a rate.

10. In an A-B-C analysis, what are antecedents and consequences?

_____

_____

_____

11. What are *specific hypotheses*?

_____

_____

_____

12. In analyzing the A-B-C information to determine hypotheses, the team should consider sociocultural factors. Discuss three cultural factors that may affect students' behavior in schools.

a. _____
_____
_____
_____

b. _____
_____
_____
_____

c. _____
_____
_____
_____
_____

13. What should the comprehensive behavioral intervention plan address?

a. _____
_____

b. _____
_____

c. _____
_____

d. _____
_____

How Can I Promote Positive Classroom Behavior in Students?

14. Discuss three of the following supports and strategies that can be used to promote the positive classroom behavior of students: affective education techniques, antecedents-based interventions, consequences-based interventions, self-management techniques, group-oriented management systems, and behavior reduction techniques.

a. _____
_____
_____
_____

b. _____

c. _____
_____
_____
_____
_____
_____
_____

How Can I Prevent Students from Harming Others?

15. Discuss some warning signs of violence and outline steps to take when violence occurs.

_____
_____
_____
_____
_____
_____
_____
_____

How Can I Adapt the Classroom Design to Accommodate Students' Learning, Social, and Physical Needs?

16. List and discuss five ways that teachers can adapt the classroom design to accommodate students' learning, social, and physical needs.

a. _____
_____
_____
_____

b. _____
_____
_____
_____
_____

c. _____
_____
_____
_____

d. _____

e. _____

Application Exercise for Chapter 7

Read "What Would You Do in Today's Diverse Classroom?" and answer the following questions.

1. How would go about assessing Victor's behavior and the environmental events that seem to be associated with it?

2. What environmental factors appear to be serving as antecedents and consequences for Victor's behavior?

3. What goals should Victor's Behavioral Intervention Plan address?

4. What strategies, curricular adaptations, and physical design modifications could be included in Victor's Behavior Intervention Plan?

5. How would you evaluate the effectiveness of Victor's Behavioral Intervention Plan?

Reflective Exercise For Chapter 7

1. What social and behavioral skills are important for success in your classroom?

2. How would you define, in observable and measurable terms, and what recording strategies would you use to assess out-of-seat, inattentive, aggressive, tardy, noisy, and disruptive behavior?

3. African American and Hispanic males and poor students receive harsher discipline for all types of behavioral offenses that their white peers and are more often suspended and physically punished (Evans & Richardson, 1995). Why do you think this is the case?

136

4. Perform a FBA on one of your behaviors, such as studying or eating. How could you use the results to change your behavior?

5. What is your opinion of block scheduling? How would it affect your teaching and your students' learning?

6. Choose a behavior you would like to increase or decrease. Select one of the self-management strategies and keep track of your progress. Were you successful? If so, why? If not, why?

7. What are some behaviors that may serve as positive, incompatible alternatives to misbehaviors such as calling out, being off task, being out of one's seat, and swearing?

For Your Information

1. Yell (1997) reviews the law concerning teacher liability for student injury and misbehavior.

2. Interviews and survey questions to identify the perspectives of teachers, students, and family members on student behavior are available (Kern-Dunlap, Clarke, & Childs, 1994; Lawry, Storey, & Danko, 1993; Lewis, Scott, & Sugai, 1994; O'Neill et al. 1997; Reid & Maag, 1998).

3. Cartledge, Kea, & Ida (2000) and Craig et al. (2000) offer reviews of culturally based student behaviors that may be misinterpreted by teachers.

4. Strategies and activities for implementing values clarification in the classroom are available (Hawley & Hawley, 1975; Howe & Howe, 1975; Simon, Howe, & Kirschenbaum, 1972).

5. Fecser and Long (1997) and Wood and Long (1990) offer guidelines on using Life Space Interviewing.

6. McCarty and Chalmers (1997) offer a list of children=s books dealing with anger.

7. A good peer mediation and conflict resolution program is the *Teaching Students to be Peacemakers Program* (Johnson & Johnson, 1996).

8. Chalmers, Olson, & Zurkowski (1999) offer guidelines for using music to foster positive classroom behavior.

9. Santos and Rettig (1999) offer guidelines for meeting the needs of students with

disabilities who attend schools that use block scheduling.

10. Allsopp, Santos, and Linn (2000) offer strategies for teaching social skills.

11. Raschke (1981) provides examples of a variety of reinforcement surveys, and Mason and Egel (1995) offer guidelines for using reinforcement surveys with students with developmental disabilities.

12. Johnson and Johnson (1999), King-Sears and Bonfil (2000), and McConnell (1999) developed guidelines for teaching students to use self-management strategies.

13. Alber and Heward (1997) provide guidelines for teaching students to recruit positive teacher attention.

14. Brody (1996) offers a list of children's literature that can be used to teach students about bullying and how to cope with it.

15. Garrity et al. (1997) have developed guidelines to help professionals, families, and students develop and use a comprehensive program to address bullying.

16. Meese (1997) offers strategies for preventing and reacting to student fights.

17. Bender and McLaughlin (1997), Webber (1997), Walker and Gresham (1997), and Embry (1997) offer suggestions and resources for making schools safer and dealing with violence, including preventing violence, and managing weapons violations and hostage situations.

18. Murdick, Gartin, and Yalowitz (1995) and Berry (1995) offer teachers pre-crisis, crisis, and post-crisis guidelines for dealing with violent behaviors.

19. Everston, Emmer, Clements, Sanford, and Worsham (1989) suggest that teachers assess classroom effectiveness by simulating their movements during a typical day, and by pretending to be a student and examining visibility, movement patterns, and accessibility of materials from the student's perspective.

20. Kolar (1996) offers suggestions to help teachers meet the seating and positioning needs of students with physical disabilities and to select wheeled mobility aids.

21. Parette and Hourcade (1986) offer guidelines for moving students forward, backward, and sideways in their wheelchairs and transferring students to toilets and the classroom floor.

SELF-TEST FOR CHAPTER 7

Directions: Select the best answer for each question. Try to answer each question, even though you might be unsure of the best answer. Remember that this is a practice test. You will not be penalized for guessing. However, before you take your class examinations, you should clarify with the instructor whether you will be penalized for guessing.

Multiple Choice Questions

1. Inconspicuous strategies that are included in the school district's policies and do not change a student's placement are:
   a. Permitted disciplinary procedures
   b. Controlled disciplinary procedures
   c. Prohibited disciplinary procedures
   d. Mandatory disciplinary procedures

2. Which is **not** a true statement about the IDEA amendments of 1997:
   a. It contains new provisions for disciplining students with disabilities
   b. It stipulates that school personnel can discipline students with and without disabilities in the same ways
   c. Students with disabilities cannot be suspended for more than 10 days
   d. If the disciplinary action of a student with disabilities relates to carrying a weapon to school, the IEP team may suspend a student indefinitely.

3. The IDEA amendment of 1997 requires that:
   a. A functional behavior assessment be conducted
   b. A behavioral intervention plan be used for students whose behaviors result in suspension
   c. The IEP team must consider positive behavioral interventions, strategies, and supports focused on the student's behavior
   d. All of the above

4. The 1997 IDEA amendments stipulated that in some cases, the IEP team can unilaterally place a student in an interim alternative setting for:
   a. More than 45 days
   b. Up to 45 days
   c. a and b
   d. None of the above

5. Which statement is **not** true about functional behavior assessment? It helps:
   a. In the development of a plan to change a student's behavior
   b. To identify strategies in which a behavior is not likely to occur
   c. To identify strategies in which a behavior is least likely to occur.
   d. Invent information to measure specific student behaviors

6. Ms. Myers is interested in measuring Carlton's out-of-seat behavior during independent seatwork activities. She defines out-of-seat behavior and decides to count the number of times Carlton is out-of-seat. What type of recording system is Ms. Myers using?
    a. Duration recording
    b. Anecdotal recording
    c. Event recording
    d. Interval recording

7. Ms. Richards wants to determine how often Dave is on-task during teacher directed instruction. After defining the behavior, she divides the 20 minute period into 20 second segments and makes a notation whether Dave was on-task or not during each 20 second segment. What type of recording system is Ms. Richards using?
    a. Event recording
    b. Time-sampling recording
    c. Duration recording
    d. Latency recording

8. This strategy views classroom misbehavior as a result of confused values:
    a. Life Space Interviewing
    b. Self-esteem probes
    c. Values clarification
    d. Three way dialogues

9. This strategy involves talking empathetically with students who are having problems in school
    a. Respectful counseling
    b. Life Space Interviewing
    c. Guidance Interviews
    d. Conflict Intervention

10. Which statement is **true** about the use of rules in the classroom?
    a. Exceptions to rules should not be discussed
    b. Teachers should have no more than 8 rules for their classroom
    c. Teachers should devise rules without input from students
    d. None of the above

11. Which statement is **false** concerning the design of behavioral contracts?
    a. Initial contracts should call for small changes in behavior
    b. Initial contracts should provide for immediate and frequent reinforcement
    c. The contract should be negotiated anytime problems arise
    d. The behavior should be stated in positive terms

12. A self-managed system whereby students verbalize to themselves the questions and responses necessary to solve problems and improve behavior is:
    a. Self-evaluation
    b. Self-instruction
    c. Self-recording
    d. Self-reinforcement

13. Ms. Palmer's students act up during reading activities. She attempts to decrease their inappropriate behaviors during reading by asking students to perform several easy tasks prior to beginning reading. Ms. Palmer is using:
    a. Differential reinforcement of incompatible behaviors
    b. Positive reinforcement
    c. Extinction
    d. Interspersed requests

14. Shirley calls out to get attention from her teacher. Her teacher decides to ignore her when she calls out. After several days, Shirley's teacher observes a decrease in her calling-out behavior. Shirley's teacher is using:
    a. Positive reinforcement
    b. Extinction
    c. Interspersed requests
    d. Response cost

True or False Questions

Directions: Read each statement carefully. Circle true if the answer is true and false, if the answer is false.

15. Latency recording and duration recording are the same
    True   False

16. Teachers should limit the number of classroom rules by using 8 rules.
    True   False

17. Permitted disciplinary procedures should not have a strongly negative impact on a student's IEP goals.
    True   False

18. Most cultures outside the U.S. view group cooperation and individualism as equally important.
    True   False

19. Life space interviewing involves talking respectfully with students who are well behaved in class.
    True   False

20. A teacher can use dialogue to help a student understand his/her behavior and work out

    alternatives to inappropriate behaviors.
    True   False

21. As a group, students can share their opinions and brainstorm solutions to class behavior problems.
    True   False

22. Classroom and school related conflicts **cannot** be handled by peer mediation.
    True   False

23. Cues cannot be used effectively to promote good classroom behavior.
    True   False

24. Reinforcers or rewards have little effect on students' behavior.
    True   False

Sentence Completion Questions

25. _____ can be used if the behavior being observed has a definite beginning and end.

26. _____ views classroom behaviors as resulting from confused values.

27. _____ involves talking empathetically with students who are having problems in school.

28. _____ are changes in the classroom events and stimuli that follow a behavior.

29. A _____ is a written agreement that outlines the behaviors and results of a specific behavior management system.

Essay Questions

30. Using examples, explain the differences among permitted disciplinary procedures, controlled disciplinary procedures, and prohibited disciplinary procedures.

31. Imagine a situation of two students fighting on the playground. Write an anecdotal record of the events that took place. Be sure to use the guidelines for writing anecdotal records.

32. Clinton, a student in your class, is exhibiting disruptive behaviors during transitions from one activity or class to another. Outline five strategies that you could employ to help Clinton adjust to transitions.

33. Prepare a schedule for a student with a disability. Discuss and give examples of the guidelines you used to develop the schedule.

Matching Question

Match the self-management strategy to its description

Description	Strategy
1. ____ Student measures his/her behavior by using a data collection system	A. Self-monitoring
2. ____ Student solves problems by verbalizing to self the questions and responses necessary to solve the problem	B. Self-evaluation
3. ____ Student evaluates his/her behavior using a rating scale and earns points based on behavior and accuracy in rating the behavior	C. Self-instruction D. Self-reinforcement
4. ____ Student then delivers reinforcement if it's appropriate	

Chapter 8: Differentiating Instruction for Diverse Learners

Chapter Overview

Chapter eight is designed to help you differentiate instruction to promote the learning of all students by accommodating their individual needs in inclusive classrooms. The chapter discusses how to use instructional technology and assistive devices to help you differentiate instruction.

Chapter Objectives

Upon completion of this chapter, students should be able to:

1. Understand how to differentiate instruction for students.
2. Employ a variety of strategies to differentiate instruction for students who have difficulty reading and gaining information from textbooks and other print materials.
3. Employ a variety of strategies to differentiate instruction for students from diverse cultural and language backgrounds.
4. Understand how to use instructional technology and assistive devices to differentiate instruction for students.

Chapter Outline

I. *Tom* (Chapter-opening vignette)
II. How Can I Differentiate Instruction for Students?
   1. Tailor Teaching Strategies to the Needs of Students and the Learning Environment
   2. Consider Students' Learning Styles
   3. Consider Students' Sensory Abilities
   4. Differentiating Instruction for Students with Visual Disabilities
   5. Differentiating Instruction for Students with Hearing Disabilities
       a. Using Educational Interpreters Effectively
       b. Maintaining Hearing Aids
   6. Consider Treatment Acceptability
   7. Use Individualized Adaptations
   8. Use Multilevel Teaching
   9. Use Curriculum Overlapping
   10. Use Tiered Assignments
   11. Use Universally Designed Instructional Materials
III. How Can I Differentiate Instruction for Students Who Have Difficulty Reading and Gaining Information from Print Materials?
   1. Use Teacher-Directed Text Comprehension Strategies

a. Previewing

b. Questioning

c. Reciprocal Teaching

d. Story-Mapping

e. POSSE

2.   Teach Student-Directed Text Comprehension Strategies

a. Finding the Main Idea

b. Surveying

c. Multipass

d. Self-Questioning

e. Paraphrasing

f. Outlining

g. Summarizing

h. Paragraph Restatements and Paragraph Shrinking

i. Critical Thinking Maps

j. Visual Imagery

k. Verbal Rehearsal

3.   Enhance the Readability of Materials

a. Highlight Essential Information

b. Use The Principles of Typographic Design

    i.   Typesize

    ii. Case

    iii. Style

    iv. Proportional and Monospaced Type

    v. Line Length

    vi. Spacing

    vii. Justification

    viii. Background

4.   Use Electronic Literacy

5.   Provide Students with Audiocassettes and Videocassettes

IV.   How Can I Differentiate Instruction for Students from Diverse Cultural and Language Backgrounds?

1.   Use a Multicultural Curriculum

a. Parallel Lessons

b. Constructive Controversy

2.   Use Multicultural Teaching Materials

3.   Use Culturally Relevant Teaching Strategies

4.   Use Reciprocal Interaction Teaching Approaches

5.   Use Effective ESL Approaches

a. Total Physical Response

b. Sheltered English

c. Natural Language Techniques

d. New Vocabulary and Concept Teaching Techniques

6.   Encourage Students to Respond

V.   How Can I Use Instructional Technology and Assistive Devices to Differentiate

Instruction for Students?
1.   Instructional Technology
   a. Computers
   b. Hypertext/Hypermedia
   c. Videocassette Recorders
   d. Videodiscs
   e. Digital Cameras
   f. CD-ROM-Based Materials
   g. Captioned Television and Liquid Crystal Display Computer Projection Panels
   h. Virtual Reality
   i. Internet
2.   Assistive Devices
   a. Devices for Students with Physical Disabilities
   b. Devices for Students with Visual and Reading Disabilities
   c. Devices for Students with Hearing Disabilities
   d. Devices for Students from Diverse Language Backgrounds

Chapter Summary

This chapter offered guidelines for differentiating instruction to address the diverse learning needs of students. Keep the following questions in mind as you review the information presented in the chapter.

a.   How Can I Differentiate Instruction for Students?
b.   How Can I Differentiate Instruction for Students Who Have Difficulty Reading and Gaining Information from Print Materials?
c.   How Can I Differentiate Instruction for Students from Diverse Cultural and Language Backgrounds?
d.   How Can I Use Instructional Technology and Assistive Devices to Differentiate Instruction for Students?

Key Terms

Learning styles	Treatment acceptability
Individualized adaptations	Multilevel teaching
Curriculum overlapping	Tiered assignments
Reciprocal teaching	Parallel lessons
Constructive controversy	Reciprocal interactive teaching approaches
Scaffolding	Total physical response

Sheltered English   Hypertext/Hypermedia

Liquid crystal display (LCD) computer   Virtual reality
projection panels

Internet   Assistive devices

Learning Activities

1. Answer these questions: How would you characterize your learning style? How do you adapt when the instructional environment does not match your learning style preference?

2. As a member of a cooperative learning group, select a textbook that matches the content and grade level in which you are most interested. Apply three text comprehension strategies to help students understand material from the textbook. Report your examples to the class.

3. Work with three classmates to design an audiocassette of a selection from a textbook or other type of printed material. Present and explain your product to the class.

4. Working as a member of a cooperative group, prepare a teacher-made material (e.g., handout, overhead, homework assignment, test, etc.) using the principles of typographic design. Present and explain your material to the class.

5. Select a program that matches the content and grade level in which you are most interested. Evaluate the software program using Hannaford and Sloane's computer software evaluation form (see text Figure 8.3) and share your results with the class.

6. Work with a small group of classmates to devise a lesson for students functioning at different levels that incorporates individualized adaptations, multi-level teaching, curriculum overlapping, tiered assignments, and universally designed instructional materials. Role play and explain your lesson to the class.

Guided Review

1. Read the vignette *Tom* and answer this question: What other instructional modifications could Ms. Taravella use to differentiate instruction for Tom and her other students?

After reading this chapter, you should be able to answer this as well as the following questions.

a. How can I differentiate instruction for students?
b. How can I differentiate instruction for students who have difficulty reading and gaining information from print materials?
c. How can I differentiate instruction for students from diverse cultural and language backgrounds?
d. How can I use instructional technology and assistive devices to differentiate instruction for students?

2. Explain what it means to differentiate instruction.

_____
_____
_____
_____
_____

How Can I Differentiate Instruction for Students?

3. Outline the seven steps of Cohen and Lynch (1991) and Arllen, Gable and Hendrickson (1996) models for selecting appropriate instructional modifications for students.

a. _____
b. _____
c. _____
d. _____
e. _____
f. _____
g. _____

4. How can you structure the classroom so that students work in their preferred style and space with respect to noise levels, proximity to others, distractions, movement, and desk arrangement?

_____
_____
_____
_____
_____

5. List characteristics of field independent learners.

_____
_____
_____

6. List characteristics of field sensitive learners.

_____
_____
_____

7. What are characteristics of field independent teachers?

_____
_____
_____

8. What are characteristics of field sensitive teachers?

_____
_____
_____

9. What is *locus of control?*

_____
_____
_____

10. How would you describe a student who has an *internal* locus of control?

_____
_____
_____

11. How would you describe a student with an *external* locus of control?

_____
_____
_____

12. A student has asked you for some examples of how to differentiate instruction for students with visual disabilities and students with hearing disabilities. What are some instructional strategies that you would provide this student?

_____
_____
_____
_____
_____
_____
_____
_____

13. What is *treatment acceptability?*

_____

_____

_____

_____

_____

14. What is involved in *individualized adaptations?*

_____

_____

_____

_____

_____

15. Collicott (1991) delineated a four-step process for designing multilevel instructional lessons. Discuss this process.

Step 1: Identification of underlying concepts.

Step 2: Consider the methods of teacher presentation.

Step 3: Consider methods of student practice and performance.

Step 4: Consider methods of evaluation.

16. The following table presents methods for differentiating instruction for students. Describe these methods.

Method	Description
1. Multilevel Teaching	
2. Curriculum Overlapping	
3. Tiered Assignments	
4. Universally Designed Materials	

How Can I Differentiate Instruction for Students Who Have Difficulty Reading and Gaining Information from Print Materials?

17. Discuss the following teacher- and student-directed strategies that can be used to promote text comprehension.

a. Previewing

b. Questioning

c. Reciprocal Teaching

d. Story Mapping

e. POSSE

18. Briefly describe the strategies to help students comprehend text that has been mentioned in this chapter.

Finding the Main Idea   Surveying
Self-Questioning   Paraphrasing
Outlining   Summarizing
Paragraph Restatements and Paragraph Shrinking   Critical Thinking Maps
Visual Imagery   Verbal Rehearsal

19. How can you increase students' comprehension of reading matter?

_____

_____

_____

20. How can you increase the readability of printed materials?

_____

_____

_____

_____

_____

21. Outline five strategies that teachers can use to adjust the linguistic complexity of text to aid students' reading comprehension.

a. _____
b. _____
c. _____
d. _____
e. _____

22. How can you increase the readability of materials?

_____

_____

_____

_____

_____

23. How do electronic books differentiate instruction for students?

_____

_____

_____

_____

_____

How Can I Differentiate Instruction for Students from Culturally and Linguistically Diverse Backgrounds?

24. What are the goals of a multicultural curriculum?

a. _____

b. _____

c. _____

d. _____

e. _____

25. Banks and Banks (1993) identified four hierarchical curricular approaches for incorporating multicultural information into existing areas. List and discuss these appoaches.

a. _____
_____

b. _____
_____

c. _____
_____

d. _____
_____

26. Parallel lessons allow students _____
_____

27. Discuss guidelines for evaluating multicultural instructional materials.

_____
_____
_____
_____
_____

28. Franklin (1992) examined the research on effective strategies for teaching students from culturally and linguistically diverse backgrounds, and identified several strategies that appear to be successful with African American students and other groups of students. List and discuss the strategies.

a. _____
_____

b. _____
_____

c. _____
_____

d. _____
_____

e.

_____

f. _____

g. _____

29. What are *reciprocal interaction teaching approaches?*

_____

_____

_____

_____

30. What do scaffolded instructional supports include?

_____

_____

_____

_____

31. Briefly discuss the following ESL approaches:

a. Total Physical Response:

b. Sheltered English:

c. Natural Language Approaches:

d. New Vocabulary and Concept Instructional Techniques:

How Can I Use Instructional Technology and Assistive Devices to Differentiate Instruction for Students?

32. Describe the following multimedia instructional technologies.
   Computers   Hypertext/Hypermedia
   Videocassette Recorders   Videodiscs
   Digital Cameras   CD-ROM-Based Materials
   Virtual Reality Systems   Internet

33. Discuss assistive devices that can be used to promote the learning, independence, and communication abilities of the following groups of students.

a. Students with Physical Disabilities

b. Students with Visual and Reading Disabilities

c. Students with Hearing Disabilities

d. Students from Linguistically Diverse Backgrounds

Application Exercise For Chapter 8

Read "What Would You Do in Today's Diverse Classroom?" and answer the following questions.

a. What process would you use to determine appropriate strategies to differentiate instruction for Alexis, Raymond, Carla, and Malik?

b. What strategies would you use to differentiate instruction for Alexis, Raymond, Carla, and Malik?

c. How could you use instructional technology and assistive devices to differentiate instruction for Alexis, Raymond, Carla, and Malik?

d. What problems might you encounter in differentiating instruction for Alexis, Raymond, Carla, and Malik?

Reflective Exercises For Chapter 8

1. How do you prefer to learn and teach? How do you adapt when the teaching strategy and environment are different from the way you prefer to learn? Should teachers match teaching to students' learning styles all of the time? Should students be taught to adapt their learning styles to the various teaching styles they will encounter in schools?

2. Think about a lesson you recently taught. How did/could you use multilevel teaching to adapt the lesson to the needs of a student with a severe disability? A student with a mild disability? A student who is gifted and talented? A second language learner?

3. Try the various text comprehension strategies using material in this textbook or in a textbook for the grade and subject matter you would like to teach. Which strategies were easiest to implement? Which ones were most effective?

4. How has your cultural background influenced your perspectives? How are your cultural perspectives similar to and different from those of others? How would multicultural education influence your cultural perspectives?

5. Watch a television show or film in a second language. What factors helped you understanding the content?

6. There continues to be a wide disparity in Internet use, with students from culturally and linguistically diverse backgrounds, lower socioeconomic groups, and single-parent families having less access to computers and the Internet (Sanger, 1999). Will this disparity create a greater gap between students? What implications would this disparity have for your use of technology to deliver instruction?

7. What teaching technologies did you use as a student? As a teacher? What were the positive and negative effects of these technologies on your learning and your students' learning?

8. What technological aids have you used to enhance your skills as a learner? To make your life easier? What have been the positive and negative impacts of using these devices?

For Your Information

1. Knowlton (1998) offers a model for designing personalized curricular supports for students with developmental disabilities.

2. Guidelines for identifying students' learning styles and designing teaching strategies and environments accordingly are available (Carbo, 1994; Dunn, 1996; Johnston, 1996).

3. Dunn, Griggs, Olson, Beasley, and Gorman (1995) and Kavale, Hirshoren, and Forness (1998) debate the research and merits of teaching based on learning styles.

4. Guidelines for using educational interpreters in schools and classrooms are available (New York State Education Department, n.d.; Salend & Longo, 1994).

5. Andrews, Winograd, and DeVille (1996) offer prereading activities for use with students who have hearing impairments and students who are second language learners.

6. Palincsar and Klenk (1991) give guidelines to prepare teachers and students to use reciprocal teaching.

7. Boyle and Weishaar (1997) have developed TRAVEL, a learning strategy to help students create cognitive organizers to facilitate their text comprehension skills.

8. Bradstad and Stumpf (1987) provide excellent guidelines for training students to learn each step involved in using SQ3R.

9. Thistlethwaite (1991) provides a six-phase model for teaching students to use summarization, and Chan (1991) offers a list of questions that students can use in creating summaries.

10. Jenkins, Heliotis, Stein, and Haynes (1987) provide guidelines for teaching students to use paragraph restatements.

11. Leigh and Lamorey (1996) offer guidelines for incorporating contemporary issues into the curriculum.

12. Santos et al. (2000) offer guidelines for selecting culturally and linguistically appropriate early childhood materials.

13. While instructional technology can enhance student learning, several concerns also have been raised (Stoll, 1995).

14. Blubaugh (1999) offers guidelines on the effectiveness of televison programs in classrooms.

15. Boone, Higgins, and Williams (1997) offer guidelines for integrating videodiscs into instructional activities.

16. Teicher (1999) presents activities, resources, and websites that can help you teach students about Internet safety and responsibility.

17. Trollinger and Slavkin (1999) describe the use of e-mail to promote the learning and socialization of a student with cognitive and behavioral disabilities.

18. Klemm (1998) offers guidelines for involving students in online conferences.

19. Peters-Walters (1998) offers guidelines for designing websites for use by individuals with disabilities.

20. Cook and Cavalier (1999) offer guidelines and a training sequence for using robotics with students.

SELF-TEST FOR CHAPTER 8

Directions: Select the best answer for each question. Try to answer each question, even though you might be unsure of the best answer. Remember that this is a practice test. You will not be penalized for guessing. However, before you take your class examinations, you should clarify with the instructor whether you will be penalized for guessing.

Multiple Choice Questions

1. Which is **not** a dimension of learning styles instruction?
    a. Environmental considerations
    b. Content-area considerations
    c. Grouping considerations
    d. Emotional considerations

2. Which is **not** a good method to differentiate instruction for students with hearing impairments?
    a. Standing still and facing the student when speaking
    b. Presenting spelling and vocabulary words in isolation
    c. Keeping the mouth area clear
    d. Using facial and body gestures

3. Mike believes that circumstances outside of his control affect his performance. He has a/an:
    a. External locus of control
    b. Internal locus of control
    c. No locus of control
    d. Developing locus of control

4. When working with a student who has as educational interpreter, a teacher should:
    a. Talk to the interpreter rather than the student
    b. Ask the interpreter to discuss the student's progress with her/his parents
    c. Have the interpreter grade the student's homework
    d. Meet with the interpreter to review curriculum and technical vocabulary

5. In Ms. Smith's class, students are given lessons in the same curriculum areas as peers but at varying levels of difficulty. This approach is referred to as:
    a. Individualized adaptations
    b. Multi-level teaching
    c. Curriculum overlapping
    d. Reciprocal interaction

6. While her classmates are working on Social Studies and Science lessons, Marie is working on following multi-step directions. This is an example of:
   a. Alternative programming
   b. Multi-level teaching
   c. Task differentiation
   d. Curriculum overlapping

7. Joan, a student with a learning disability in Ms. Duncan's class, is permitted to display her learning of a story she read by writing a book report, designing a book jacket, writing a play, drawing a picture, composing a poem, or making a video. Ms. Duncan is using:
   a. Tiered assignments
   b. Curriculum overrlapping
   c. Reciprocal interactions
   d. Individualized adaptations

8. Before teaching a new reading lesson, Mr. Watt instructs his students to preview the new vocabulary words, scan the passage, and discuss the meaning of bold-faced terms. Which strategy is Mr. Watt using?
   a. Reviewing
   b. Previewing
   c. Reciprocal teaching
   d. Curriculum overlapping

9. Ms. Ellis helps her students to identify the structure and major elements of a story by using a visual representation of the major elements. Ms. Ellis is using:
   a. Guided reading
   b. Semantic feature analysis
   c. Reciprocal teaching
   d. Story-mapping

10. A series of strategies that a teacher uses before, during, and after reading text to promote comprehension is referred to as:
    a. POSSE
    b. Hypertext
    c. Surveying
    d. Guided reading

11. This is a modified version of SQ3R:
    a. Multi-level teaching
    b. Interpersonal teaching
    c. Multipass
    d. Self-questioning

12. Which statement is **false** about videodiscs? They:
    a. Allow students to hear explanations
    b. Allow students to view colorful animated and expressive visual displays
    c. Are cost effective
    d. All of the above

13. Ms. Hermitt has her students communicate with students in other parts of the country through computerized chat groups. What instructional technology is Ms. Hermitt using?
    a. Virtual reality
    b. Internet
    c. CD-ROM
    d. LCD panel

14. An adaptive device that can help students with visual impairments acquire information from print material is:
    a. Mowat Sensor Reader
    b. Laser Disc Decoder
    c. Telecommunication Reading Device
    d. Kurzweil 3000

True or False Questions

Directions: Read each statement carefully. Circle true if the answer is true, and false if the answer is false.

15. Field independent teachers tend to employ personal and conversational instructional techniques.
    True   False

16. The effects of acculturation may cause students to exhibit behaviors that are indicative of an external locus of control.
    True   False

17. In preparing cassettes for students, it is often helpful for the speaker to read at a rate of 120–175 words per minute.
    True   False

18. Assistive devices can help individuals with disabilities organize and take notes.
    True   False

19. TTY or TDD allows individuals with visual impairments to communicate.
    True   False

Sentence Completion Questions

20. A student's belief about the relationship between effort and achievement is referred to as _____.

21. The extent to which one views a specific teaching strategy as easy to use, effective, appropriate for the setting, fair, and reasonable is _____.

22. _____ are particularly effective in promoting recall by establishing the need for review.

23. In _____, students pause after reading several sentences to themselves and verbalize to themselves the selection's content.

24. A teacher can make the curriculum multicultural by using _____, which allow students to learn about individuals and content from both the mainstream culture and other cultures.

Essay Questions

25. Identify and discuss six strategies for adapting instruction for students with visual disabilities.

26. Teresa, a student who needs an educational interpreter, is going to be placed in your class. Discuss how you would coordinate responsibilities with and orient the educational interpreter.

27. You have been selected to be a member of your school's instructional technology and multimedia committee. Outline and describe four types of instructional technology and multimedia you would like educators to use. Discuss how educators might use these technologies to instruct students.

28. Franklin examined the research on effective strategies for teaching students from culturally and linguistically diverse backgrounds, and identified seven strategies that

appear to be successful with African American students. Identify, discuss, and give examples of four of the seven strategies Franklin examined.

Matching Question

Match the alternative keyboarding device with its description.

Description	Device
1. _____ An array of letters, phrases, and numerals are displayed on the screen which the student selects through the use of switch	A. Graphics tablet
2. _____ A device which activates the computer when it touches the screen	B. Joystick
3. _____ A small slate covered with templates of pictures, words, and numerals which may be entered into the computer when touched by a stylus	C. Scanning systems
4. _____ A device that modifies the size and spacing of the keys on the keyboard	D. Key guard
5. _____ A device that is moved in different directions to control the cursor	E. Light pen

Chapter 9: Differentiating Large- and Small-Group Instruction for Diverse Learners

Chapter Overview

Chapter nine provides strategies for fostering learning when using large- and small-group instruction for all students. The chapter includes strategies on how to use the principles of effective teaching and cooperative learning.

Chapter Objectives

Upon completion of this chapter, students should be able to:

1. Discuss the factors and procedures which planning teams and teachers should consider in differentiating instruction for students.
2. Employ a variety of strategies to differentiate large-group instruction to address the learning needs of students.
3. Understand how to teach effectively.
4. Understand how to successfully use cooperative learning arrangements with students.

Chapter Outline

I. *Mr. Armstrong* (Chapter-opening vignette)
II. How Can I Adapt Large-Group Instruction for Students?
    1. Have Students Work Collaboratively
        a. Collaborative Discussion Teams
        b. Send a Problem
        c. Numbered Heads Together
        d. Think-Pair-Share
        e. Bookends
    2. Use Presentation Software/Overhead Projector
    3. Encourage Students to Ask Questions
    4. Help Students Take Notes
        a. Outlines
        b. Highlighting Main Points
        c. Peer Note Takers and Audiocassette Recorders
    5. Teach Note-Taking Skills and Strategies
    6. Foster Students' Listening Skills
        a. Motivating Students to Listen
        b. Paraphrasing
        c. Using cues

Chapter Summary

This chapter offered guidelines for differentiating large- and small-group instruction to meet the unique learning needs of students. As you review the chapter, keep the following questions in mind.

a. How Can I Adapt Large Group Instruction for Students?
b. How Can I Use Effective Instruction to Teach Students?
c. How Can I Successfully Use Cooperative Learning Arrangements with Students?

Key Terms

Collaborative discussion teams

Presentation software/Overhead projector

Cooperative learning arrangements

Effective teaching

Learning Activities

1. Perform a task analysis. You might task analyze a motor skill that has a discrete sequence of steps or you might task analyze an academic skill.

2. Plan a set of directions incorporating the strategies for helping students follow directions.

3. Develop a vignette depicting a student who is not performing up to his or her ability because of problems with motivation. Ask the class to brainstorm possible strategies for motivating the student depicted in the vignette.

4. Work in a cooperative learning group to develop and present to the class a cooperative academic game. The class should provide feedback to the group concerning the rules, prerequisite skills, cooperative goal structures, academic content, and other game variables.

5. Copy a page of a textbook. Highlight information from the copy applying the guidelines for highlighting information in the textbook. Share your products with the class.

Guided Review

1. Read the vignette, *Mr. Armstrong*, and answer the following question:

a. What other instructional adaptations could Mr. Armstrong use to differentiate instruction for students?

After reading the chapter, you should be able to answer this as well as the following questions.

a. How can I adapt large-group instruction for students?
b. How can I use effective instruction to teach students?
c. How can I successfully use cooperative learning arrangements with students?

How Can I Adapt Large-Group Instruction for Students?

2. Discuss the following strategies that teachers can use to foster collaboration among students.

a. Collaborative Discussion Teams:

_____

_____

_____

_____

_____

b. Send a Problem:

_____

_____

_____

_____

_____

c. Numbered Heads Together:

_____

_____

_____

_____

_____

d. Think-Pair-Share:

_____

_____

_____

_____
_____
_____

e. Bookends:

_____
_____
_____
_____
_____

3. Discuss how you can use the following to differentiate large group instruction for students.

a. Use Presentation Software/Overhead Projector:

_____
_____
_____
_____
_____

b. Encourage Students to Ask Questions

_____
_____
_____
_____
_____

4. Some students in your class are experiencing difficulty taking notes. Briefly discuss three strategies that you can use to help them improve their note-taking skills?

a. _____
    _____

b. _____
    _____

c. _____
    _____

5. What note-taking skills and strategies could you recommend to a student to improve his or her note taking?

_____
_____
_____
_____
_____

6. Discuss the following five strategies that can be used to foster students' listening skills.

a. Motivating Students to Listen:

b. Paraphrasing:

c. Using cues:

d. Screening:

e. Listening Materials:

7. How can you gain and maintain students' attention?

_____

_____

_____

_____

How Can I Use Effective Instruction?

8. List and briefly discuss the elements of effective teaching.

a. Element 1: Establish the Lesson's Purpose by Explaining Its Goals and Objectives

b. Element 2: Review Prerequisite Skills

c. Element 3: Use Task Analysis and Introduce Content in Separate Steps Followed by Practice

d. Element 4: Give Clear Directions, Explanations, and Relevant Examples

e. Element 5: Provide Time for Active and Guided Practice

f. Element 6: Promote Active Responding and Check for Understanding Questioning

g. Element 7: Give Prompt, Specific Feedback

h. Element 8: Offer Time for Independent Activities

i. Element 9: Summarize Main Points and Evaluate Mastery

How Can I Successfully Use Cooperative Learning Arrangements with Students?

9.   Briefly discuss ten ways to use cooperative learning arrangements with students.

a.   b.

c.   d.

e.   f.

g.   h.

i.   j.

Application Exercise For Chapter 9

Read "What Would You Do In Today's Diverse Classroom?" and answer the following questions.

a. What problem(s) are you encountering in each situation?

b. What would you do to address the situation?

c. What resources and support would you need to implement strategies to address the situation?

Reflective Exercises for Chapter 9

1. What strategies do your instructors use to facilitate your note taking in class?

2. What skills and strategies do you use to pay attention and take notes in class? Are they successful? How do they compare with the strategies presented in this book?

3. How would you task analyze a motor skill such as brushing your teeth? How would you task analyze a cognitive skill such as measuring a line using a ruler?

4. Identify a game you or your students like to play. How can you apply the principles presented here to make this game cooperative?

For Your Information

1. Lazarus (1996) offers guidelines for developing and using skeleton guided notes.

2. Strategies that can help students take notes include CALL UP and "A" NOTES (Czarnecki, Rosko & Fine, 1998), and LINKS and AWARE (Suritsky & Hughes, 1996).

3. Anderson-Inman, Knox-Quinn, and Horney (1996) offer guidelines for using computer-based study strategies to take notes in class and from textbooks.

4. Rademacher, Cowart, Sparks, and Chism (1997) have developed the Quality Assignment Planning Worksheet and the Assignment Idea Chart to help you plan and use lessons that motivate your students.

5. Hertzog (1998a) offers guidelines for using open-ended learning activities.

6. Margolis (1999) has developed *Student Motivation: A Problem Solving Questionnaire* to help use, analyze, and promote student motivation.

7. Blum and Yocom (1996) offer guidelines for designing academic learning games to use in inclusive settings.

8. Heward et al. (1996) offer guidelines for developing and using preprinted and write-on response cards.

9. Rademacher (2000) offers strategies for involving students in completing and evaluating their independent assignments.

10. Olympia, Andrews, Valum, and Jenson (1993) developed a program to give teachers guidelines for using cooperative homework teams.

11. Longwill and Kleinert (1998) offer guidelines for setting up a high school peer tutoring program.

12. Dishon and O'Leary (1991) offer guidelines for assigning students to heterogeneous cooperative groups.

13. Goodwin (1992), Kagan (1992) and Goor and Schwenn (1993) offer team-building activities to help students get to know each other and develop cooperative skills, and Vernon, Schumaker, and Deshler (1995) have developed the Cooperative Strategies Series to teach students cooperative and teamwork skills.

SELF-TEST FOR CHAPTER 9

Directions: Select the best answer for each question. Try to answer each question, even though you might be unsure of the best answer. Remember that this is a practice test. You will not be penalized for guessing. However, before you take your class examinations, you should clarify with the instructor whether you will be penalized for guessing.

Multiple Choice Questions

1. Which of the following cooperative learning arrangements is **not** used to help students gain information from a teacher-directed oral presentation?
   a. Collaboration Discussion Teams
   b. Learning Together
   c. Numbered Heads Together
   d. Think-Pair-Share

2. Which of these has **not** been presented as a strategy for motivating students to learn?
   a. Facial expressions
   b. High-pitched voice
   c. Voice changes
   d. Gestures

3. Which statement is **not** true about peer note takers? They:
   a. Always take notes outside of class
   b. Should master the subject matter
   c. Use carbon paper or photocopy machines
   d. Are sensitive to students who need help

4. Which of the following is **not** a student note-taking skill?
   a. Reviewing and editing notes
   b. Indicating overlaps between the textbook and the teacher's comments
   c. Recording the length of time spent on a topic
   d. All of the above

5. Mr. Wilson uses an activity relating to his students' interests to introduce a new lesson and to motivate them to learn the material. This is an example of:
   a. Screening
   b. Adult-directed teaching
   c. Anticipatory set
   d. Instructive teaching

6. Which of the following statements is **true**. When giving directions orally, the teacher should:
   a. Use complex vocabulary
   b. Cut down on unnecessary words
   c. Use consistent terms from assignment to assignment
   d. Ensure that all students are attentive

7. Which of the following is **not** considered an alternative method to promote higher-order thinking and problem-solving abilities?
   a. Reciprocal interaction teaching approaches
   b. Cooperative learning
   c. Technology-based instruction
   d. Multi-formatted approaches

8. When using questions, you should allow students:
   a. At least 5-10 seconds to formulate their answers
   b. At least 2 seconds to respond
   c. More than 2 minutes to respond
   d. Two seconds to respond

9. Mr. Jones offers feedback that guides his students on how to perform a task. Mr. Jones is using:
   a. General feedback
   b. Prompting
   c. Corrective feedback
   d. Process feedback

10. In cooperative learning arrangements, an understanding that each group member is responsible for contributing to the group and learning the material is referred to as:
    a. Positive interdependence
    b. Group processing
    c. Individual accountability
    d. All of the above

11. A cooperative learning format that combines cooperatively structured learning with individualized instruction is:
    a. Student Teams-Achievement Divisions
    b. Jigsaw
    c. Group Project
    d. Team-Assisted Instruction

12. Which of the following is **not** a cooperative learning evaluation format?
    a. Group project/Group grade
    b. Jigsaw grade
    c. Contract grading
    d. Group average

13. Which of the following is **not** a goal of homework?
    a. Teach independent study skills
    b. Communicate to parents the skills that are being covered in school
    c. Introduce students to new skills
    d. Complete work not finished in school

14. Teachers can help students gain information from oral presentations by:
    a. Using jokes and humorous anecdotes
    b. Stating the relevance of the oral presentation
    c. Explaining prerequisite information
    d. All of the above

True or False Questions

Directions: Read each statement carefully. Circle true if the answer is true, and false if the answer is false.

15. Think-Pair-Share is a cooperative learning strategy that can help students master content presented orally.
    True   False

16. You can examine your success in giving oral presentations to students by using ordinal numbers and time cues to organize information.
    True   False

17. To help students determine important points to include in their notes, you can use introductory phrases and a monotonous voice.
    True   False

18. Whether students are using peer note takers or audiocassettes, they can be required to take notes during class.
    True   False

19. Paraphrasing skills can be taught by asking students to paraphrase peer comments.
    True   False

20. Research has shown that verbal and nonverbal cues do not improve students' listening skills.
    True   False

21. Some researchers have noted that students' listening skills can be improved by using a cue card that lists the guidelines for listening.
    True   False

22. Students cannot be taught how to respond to verbal cues.
    True   False

23. Many children do **not** have difficulty focusing their attention on school-related tasks.
    True   False

24. In presenting directions that have several steps, you can number and list the steps in order.
    True   False

Sentence Completion Questions

25. _____ is established when students understand that they must work together to achieve their goals.

26. _____ is a systematic process of stating and sequencing the parts of a task to determine what subtasks must be performed in order to master the task.

27. _____ interactions occur when students encourage and help each other learn the material.

28. In _____, each member of the group is given a specific role.

29. _____ is an evaluation format in which groups contract for a grade based on the amount of work they agree to do based upon a set of criteria.

Essay Questions

30. Bill, a student in your class, is having difficulty gaining information from oral presentations. Outline five strategies you could use to modify your oral presentations to help Bill.

31. Task analyze the skill of using a ruler to measure the length of a line.

32. Identify and discuss four problems teachers may encounter when using cooperative learning arrangements. Describe at least one solution for each of these problems.

33. You notice that several of your students' work areas and notebooks are cluttered and disorganized. Outline five strategies that you could use to assist students in organizing their work areas and notebooks.

Matching Questions

Applying what you have read about listening strategies, match the listening strategy with its description.

Description	Listening Strategy
1. ____ Students seek clarification of verbally presented materials.	A. Paraphrasing
2. ____ Students are reminded to listen and to pay attention.	B. Questioning
3. ____ Students convert the message of the speaker to their own words.	C. Screening
4. ____ Students identify relevant from non-essential information.	D. Cues

Chapter 10: Differentiating Reading, Writing, and Spelling Instruction

Chapter Overview

In addition to differentiating instruction for diverse learners and teaching that involves the use of large and small groups, teachers need to help students develop literacy skills. This chapter offers guidelines for teaching and differentiating instruction so that you can help all students learn to read, write, and spell.

Chapter Objectives

Upon completion of this chapter, students should be able to:

1. Employ a variety of approaches and strategies to teach and adapt reading instruction.
2. Employ a variety of approaches and strategies to teach and adapt writing instruction.
3. Employ a variety of approaches and strategies to teach and adapt spelling instruction.

Chapter Outline

I.   *Ms. Pike* (Chapter-opening vignette)
II.   How Can I Help Students Learn to Read?
    1.   Motivate Students to Read
    2.   Use a Balanced Approach
        a. Phonetic Approaches
        b. Whole Word Approaches
            i. Basal Readers
        c. Language Experience Approach
        d. Whole Language Approach
            i. Components of Whole Language Programs
            ii. Whole Language Curricular Adaptations
    3.   Use Remedial Reading Strategies
        a. Cooperative Integrated Reading and Composition
        b. Reading Recovery
        c. Multisensory Strategies
            i. Fernald Method
            ii. Orton-Gillingham-Stillman Strategy

4.   Use Programmed Reading Materials
5.   Employ Cueing Strategies
     a. Language Cues
     b. Visual Cues
     c. Physical Cues
     d. Configuration Cues
     e. Context Cues
         i. Syntactic Cues
         ii. Semantic Cues
         iii. Pictorial Cues
6.   Involve Families

III.   How Can I Help Students Learn to Write?
1.   Make Writing Meaningful and an Integral Part of the Curriculum
     a. Use Journals
2.   Use a Process-Oriented Approach to Writing Instruction
     a. Planning/Prewriting
         i. Idea Generation
     b. Drafting
     c. Editing And Revising
         i. Proofreading
         ii. Models
         iii. Collaborative Writing Groups
         iv. Writers' Workshop
     d. Publishing
         i. Feedback
3.   Teach Students to Use Learning Strategies
4.   Employ Computer-Supported Writing Applications
     a. Word Processing
     b. Spell Checkers
     c. Word Cueing and Prediction
     d. Text Organization, Grammar, and Punctuation Assistance

IV.   How Can I Help Students Learn to Spell?
1.   Use a Combination of Approaches
     a. Rule-Governed Approaches
     b. Cognitive Approaches
     c. Whole Word Approaches
         i. Test-Study-Test Procedures
         ii. Corrected-Test Methods
         iii. Word Study Techniques
2.   Adapt Spelling Instruction
     a. Explain the Importance of Spelling
     b. Teach Dictionary Skills
     c. Teach Students to Proofread and to Correct Spelling Errors

d. Use Spelling Games
e. Use Computer Programs
f. Teach Students to Use Cues
g. Have Students Record Their Progress and Correct Their Own Spelling Errors
h. Provide Time to Review Words Previously Learned
i. Model Appropriate Spelling Techniques
j. Teach Useful Prefixes, Suffixes, and Root Words

Chapter Summary

This chapter presented guidelines and strategies for differentiating reading, writing, and spelling instruction. Try to remember the information to answer the following questions:

a. How can I help students learn to read?
b. How can I help students learn to write?
c. How can I help students learn to spell?

Key Terms

Balanced approach	Phonetic approaches
Whole word approaches	Language experience approach
Whole language approach	Cooperative integrated reading and composition
Reading recovery	Multisensory strategies
Programmed reading materials	Process-oriented approach
Word processing	Word cueing and prediction
Rule governed approaches	Cognitive approaches
Whole word approaches	

Learning Activities

1. Working in a cooperative learning group, develop a reading lesson using one of the following reading approaches: synthetic phonetic approach, analytic phonetic approach, linguistic approach, whole word approach, basal reader system, whole language approach, and language experience approach. Present your lesson to the class. Discuss the differences in the lessons and the approaches.

2. Work with three classmates to adapt a reading lesson for second language learners. Discuss the curricular adaptations you employed with the class.

3. Work with some of your classmates to develop a lesson using Cooperative Integrated Reading and Composition (CIRC). Present your lesson to the class.

4. Work with a classmate to role play a student reading to a teacher. The reader should periodically make errors and the teacher should attempt to aid the student by applying a variety of teacher and student cues and other error correction techniques. Ensure that each dyad member has the opportunity to perform both roles. At the end of the role play, ask each dyad to discuss the cues and error correction techniques they used.

5. Work with a small group of classmates to write a story using a process-oriented approach. Structure the task so that you go through each step in the process: planning, drafting, revising, editing, and publishing. Share your product and discuss how your group collaborated throughout the process.

6. Divide the class into small groups. Ask each group to develop a spelling lesson using one of the spelling approaches: linguistic approach, phonetic approach, cognitive approach, test-study-test procedure, corrected test method, and word study techniques.

Guided Review

1. Read *Ms. Pike,* the chapter-opening vignette, and answer the following question.

a. What strategies are being used by Ms. Pike using to promote the literacy skills of her students?

After reading this chapter, you should be able to answer this as well as the following questions.

a. How can I help students learn to read?
b. How can I help students learn to write?

c. How can I help students learn to spell?

How Can I Help Students Learn to Read?

2. Several approaches are available to help students learn to read. Select six of the approaches and briefly discuss how you would use them to help students develop their reading skill.

a. _____
_____
_____

b. _____
_____
_____

c. _____
_____
_____

d. _____
_____
_____

e. _____
_____
_____

f. _____
_____
_____

3. Match the reading approach with its description.

Reading Approach	Description
A. Phonetic B. Whole Word C. Orton-Gillingham-Stillman D. Language Experience E. Basal Readers F. Fernald G. Whole Language	_____ Involves four steps: tracing, writing without tracing, recognition in print, and word analysis _____ Introduces complex words gradually as students progress through the series _____ Emphasizes reading for meaning rather than learning decoding skills in isolation _____ Employs a multisensory synthetic phonics approach to teaching reading _____ Focuses on helping students learn to blend and segment sounds within words _____ Is based on the belief that what students think about, they can talk about

4. List and briefly describe four cueing strategies that teachers can use to help students learn difficult or unfamiliar words.

a. _____
_____
_____

b. _____
_____
_____

c. _____
_____
_____

d. _____
_____
_____

How Can I Help Students Learn to Write?

5. Several approaches are available to help students develop their writing skill. Select and discuss six of these approaches.

a. _____
_____
_____
_____

b. _____
_____
_____
_____

c. _____
_____
_____
_____

d. _____
_____
_____
_____

e. _____
_____
_____
_____

f. _____
_____
_____
_____

6. Identify four limitations in using spell checkers.

a. _____
_____

b. _____
_____

c. _____
_____

d. _____
_____

7. Ashton (1998) developed the CHECK procedure, a mnemonic learning strategy designed to assist students in using spell checkers. Discuss the steps in the CHECK procedure.

C

H

E

C

K

How Can I Help Students Learn to Spell?

8. Students who have difficulty in spelling may benefit from a spelling program that combines several of the approaches presented in this chapter. Select and discuss two of these approaches.

a. _____
_____
_____
_____
_____
_____
_____

b. _____
_____
_____
_____
_____
_____
_____

Application Exercise For Chapter 10

Read "What Would You Do In Today's Diverse Classroom?" and answer the following questions.

a. What would you do to help Richard learn to read?

b. What would you do to help Richard learn to write?

c. What would you do to help Richard learn to spell?

d. What resources and support from others would be helpful to you in helping Richard learn to read, write, and spell?

Reflective Exercises for Chapter 10

1. How could you use cues to help students who have difficulty reading the following words: *laugh, bee, floor, eat, yellow, jump, seven, quiet, why, and small*?

2. What cueing strategies do you use when you encounter a word you don't know? When working with students?

3. How did you learn to write? When you write a paper for class or a letter to a friend, what processes do you use? How does the use of a computer and word processing affect your writing?

4. What approaches did your teachers use to teach you spelling? What were the strengths of these approaches? What were their weaknesses?

For Your Information

1. Sanacore (1999) offers guidelines for reading aloud to students.

2. Chard and Dickson (1999), Edelen-Smith (1997), Mathes et al. (1999), and Smith (1998) present assessment techniques, training programs, and teaching strategies to assess and promote the phonemic awareness of students.

3. Chard and Osborn (1999) offer guidelines and activities for using a phonetic approach to teach letter-sound correspondence, regular and irregular words, story reading, and word analysis.

4. Lebzelter and Nowacek (1999) describe two learning strategies, DISSECT and WIST (Word Identification Strategy Training), that you can teach to your students to help them decode words.

5. Bryant, Ugel, Thompson, & Hamff (1999) offer activities for teaching word identification, vocabulary, and comprehension.

6. Alber (1996) offers guidelines for creating interest, holding students accountable, and preventing disruptions during sustained silent reading.

7. Keefe (1995a) offers guidelines for using literature circles to create a community of readers in the classroom.

8. Pike, Compain, and Mumper (1994) offer guidelines and examples of thematic units that integrate reading, writing, and content area learning, as well as suggestions for organizing the classroom to promote the use of a whole language approach.

9. Bligh (1996) and Perry (1997) offer guidelines for using picture books and provide a bibliography of recommended picture books.

10. Calderon, Hertz-Lazarowitz, and Tinajero (1991) adapted the CIRC model for use in multiethnic and bilingual classrooms.

11. Salembier and Cheng (1997) have developed SCUBA-DIVE, a learning strategy that helps students use six different cues to decode unfamiliar words.

12. Kluwin (1996) describes how to use dialogue journals to encourage students working in dyads to write to each other.

13. Ellis (1997) outlines the steps in POWER, a learning strategy that can be used to prompt students to use a writing process approach.

14. Graham (1992) describes a strategy to help students establish writing goals by teaching them to use a planning strategy called *PLANS*.

15. Strategies such as *DEFENDS, TOWER, PENS, SEARCH,* and *WRITER* can be employed to monitor the quality of students' writing (Ellis & Covert, 1996; Mercer & Mercer, 1993).

16. Isaacson and Gleason (1998) offer a variety of strategies to assess students' written language, and McAlister, Nelson, and Bahr (1999) offer strategies for assessing students' understanding of and attitudes toward a writing process approach.

17. Other learning strategies that can be taught to students include TREE (Sexton, Harris, & Graham, 1998), PLAN and WRITE (De La Paz, 1999), STOP and DARE (De La Paz & Graham, 1997), and STOP and LIST (Troia, Graham, & Harris, 1999).

18. McNaughton, Hughes, and Ofiesh (1997) developed INSPECT, a learning strategy to teach students to use a spell checker.

19. Sturm et al. (1997) offer guidelines for selecting appropriate software for computer-assisted writing.

20. Smith, Boone and Higgins (1998) offer guidelines for using the Internet as part of the writing process.

21. Richards and Gipe (1993) offer a variety of spelling activities that you can use to integrate spelling into your language arts programs.

SELF-TEST FOR CHAPTER 10

Directions: Select the best answer for each question. Try to answer each question, even though you might be unsure of the best answer. Remember that this is a practice test. You will not be penalized for guessing. However, before you take your class examinations, you should clarify with the instructor whether you will be penalized for guessing.

1. A teacher is teaching reading by having students learn to read and spell word families that share the same phonetic patterns. The teacher is using a/an:
   a. Synthetic phonetic approach
   b. Analytic phonetic approach
   c. Whole language approach
   d. Linguistic approach

2. Students who are taught to read using a whole word approach tend to:
   a. Attempt to read unfamiliar words
   b. Use context cues
   c. Substitute familiar words for new words
   d. All of the above

3. Which of the following are visual cues?
   a. Color cues
   b. Size cues
   c. Graphic cues
   d. All of the above

4. Which of the following statements is an accurate description of simulated journals?
   a. Students take and write about the perspective of another person
   b. Teachers assign students to write about their experiences
   c. Students maintain a written conversation with one of their classmates
   d. None of the above

5. The collaboration writing model that allows one group member to transform the contributions of individual group members into a larger group draft is the:
   a. Author's chair model
   b. Raisin bread model
   c. Peer-revising model
   d. All of the above

6. Which of the following curricular adaptations is appropriate for students who are second language learners?
   a. Recursive encounters
   b. Choral reading
   c. Storytelling
   d. All of the above

7. When her students misread words, Ms. Thompson mimes the distinct qualities or actions associated with the words. Ms. Thompson uses:
   a. Physical cues
   b. Visual cues
   c. Configurative cues
   d. Dramatic cues

8. A dialogue journal involves:
   a. Students and teachers writing responses to each other
   b. Students writing the dialogue of a daily event
   c. Students writing the dialogue of imaginary events
   d. Students writing dialogue with their peers

9. Some students are having difficulty planning their writing assignments. You could help them in this phase of writing by using:
   a. Choral reading
   b. Story enders
   c. Neurological impress
   d. Word supply

10. Students can work in collaborative writing groups by:
    a. Brainstorming ideas for writing
    b. Editing the products of peers
    c. Developing group outlines
    d. All of the above

True or False Questions

Directions: Read each statement carefully. Circle true if the answer is true, and false if the answer is false.

11. Instruction in phonics is an essential component of a whole language approach to teaching reading.
    True   False

12. In the basal series, vocabulary and new skills are introduced in a gradual, logical sequence.
    True   False

13. Directed reading includes three components: preparation, reading, and discussion.
    True   False

14. In the phonetic approach, the emphasis is on reading for meaning.
    True   False

15. When using a whole language approach, a teacher can use a variety of teaching strategies and curricular adaptations.
    True   False

16. Research has revealed that configuration cues are highly effective.
    True   False

17. Context clues are not very useful in determining the pronunciation of unknown words.
    True   False

18. Thompson and Taymans developed the FIGURE learning strategy to teach students how to use context clues.
    True   False

19. Students with disabilities may encounter problems using word processing.
    True   False

20. Editing groups allow editing to be done by the individual student rather than by the group.
    True   False

Sentence Completion Questions

21. The _____ approach develops phonetic skills by teaching students the specific symbol-grapheme correspondence rules.

22. A _____ approach is based on the belief that what student think, they can talk about; what students can say, they can write or have someone write for them; and what students can write, they can read.

23. Through _____, students can act out and retell stories through miming, gestures, role playing, and the use of props.

24. A program that uses basal readers, direct instruction, integrated reading and writing, and cooperative learning to teach reading and writing skills is referred to as

    _____.

25. _____ teach letters and words using combinations of visual, auditory, kinesthetic, and tactile modalities.

Essay Questions

26. Differentiate between analytic and synthetic phonetic approach.

27. Define and give examples of three types of teacher cues and five types of student cues.

28. Discuss two ways teachers can make writing meaningful.

29. List and describe the steps in a process-oriented approach to teaching writing.

Matching Questions

Match the teaching sequence of the cooperative integrated reading and composition program with its description.

Description	Listening Strategy
1. _____ Students work as a team to respond to comprehensive questions, and produce a written product.	A. Partner Reading
2. _____ Teachers offer students direct instruction on writing strategies and specific language arts objectives.	B. Story-related Writing
3. _____ Partners sign an assignment sheet to indicate that their peers have completed the task(s) successfully.	C. Words out loud D. Partner checking
4. _____ When one student is reading, the other is listening and offering feedback.	E. Integrated language arts
5. _____ Students work in dyads to learn to read and define a list of new or difficult words from the story.	

Chapter 11: Differentiating Mathematics, Science, and Social Studies Instruction

Chapter Overview

Many strategies for differentiating classroom instruction to enhance learning, motivation, and social development can be used across academic discipline. Chapter eleven presents ways to adapt content area instruction to help all students learn by providing guidelines for differentiating mathematics, science, and social studies instruction.

Chapter Objectives

Upon completion of this chapter, students should be able to:

1. Employ a variety of approaches to differentiate mathematics instruction.
2. Employ a variety of approaches to differentiate science and social studies instruction.
3. Employ a variety of strategies to differentiate social studies instruction.
4. Create a multicultural curriculum and use multicultural materials that are meaningful for all students.

Chapter Outline

I. *Ms. Hofbart* (Chapter-opening vignette)
II. How Can I Differentiate Mathematics Instruction?
    1. Use a Problem Solving Approach
    2. Present Mathematics Appropriately
       a. Organize Instruction to Follow a Developmental Sequence
       b. Introduce Concepts and Present Problems Through Everyday Situations
       c. Teach the Language of Mathematics
    3. Use Teaching Aids
       a. Teach Students to Use Manipulatives and Concrete Teaching Aids
       b. Use Visuals to Illustrate Concepts, Problems, Solutions, and Inter-relationships
       c. Use Instructional Technology and Teach Students to Use It
       d. Encourage and Teach Students to Use Calculators
    4. Use a Variety of Instructional Approaches
       a. Use Peer-Mediated Instruction

        b. Use Mathematics Programs and Curriculums to Guide and Support Instruction

        c. Offer Students Specialized Instruction in Solving Word Problems

        d. Teach Students to Use Self-Management Techniques and Learning Strategies

        e. Give Students Models, Cues, and Prompts

    5. Help Students Develop Their Math Facts and Computation Skills

        a. Vary the Instructional Sequence

        b. Promote Mastery and Automaticity

        c. Use Remedial Programs

        d. Match Instruction to Students' Error Types

    6. Provide Feedback and Use Assessment to Guide Future Teaching

        a. Offer Prompt Feedback

        b. Involve Students in the Assessment Process

III. How Can I Differentiate Science and Social Studies Instruction?

    1. Choose and Use Appropriate Instructional Materials

        a. Choose Textbooks Carefully

        b. Consider Electronic Textbooks

        c. Teach Students How to Use Textbooks and Instructional Materials

            i. Note Taking from Textbooks

        d. Use Study Guides

        e. Use Adapted Textbooks and Parallel Alternative Curriculum

    2. Use Content Enhancements

        a. Advance and Post Organizers

            i. Graphic Organizers

            ii. Semantic Webs

            iii. Anticipation Guides

            iv. Concept-Teaching Routines

    3. Use a Variety of Instructional Approaches and Practices

        a. Use Activities-Oriented Approaches

        b. Organize Instruction Around Big Ideas and Interdisciplinary Themes

        c. Relate Instruction to Students' Lives and General Societal Problems

        d. Use Effective Questioning Techniques

        e. Use Specially Designed Programs and Curriculums

        f. Improve Students' Memory

            i. Key Word Method

        g. Use Instructional Technology and Multimedia

        h. Take Students on Field Trips

    4. Address the Needs of Diverse Learners

Chapter Summary

This chapter presented guidelines and strategies for differentiating mathematics, science, and social studies instruction. As you review the chapter, consider the following questions:

a. How Can I Differentiate Mathematics Instruction?
b. How Can I Differentiate Science and Social Studies Instruction?

Key Terms

Manipulatives

Peer mediated instruction

Learning strategies

Study guides

Parallel alternative curriculum

Instructional technology

Self-management techniques

Computation skills

Advance and post organizers

Instructional approaches and practices

Learning Activities

1. Work with a few classmates to develop and present a mathematics lesson using the problem-solving principles presented in the chapter. Present your lesson to the class and share how you incorporated the problem-solving principles for teaching mathematics.

2. Develop three word problems and describe five ways you could assist students in solving each of the word problems.

3. Research and take to class a remedial math program that can be used to teach students.

4. Select a science or social studies textbook that matches the grade level in which you are most interested. Adapt the content in the textbook for students using three of the following: advance and post organizers, graphic organizers, semantic webs, anticipation guides, and concept teaching routines. Ask each group to share their product with the class.

5. Work in a cooperative group to evaluate a social studies or science textbook using the guidelines presented in the chapter. Examine how the textbook portrays females and individuals from culturally and linguistically diverse backgrounds. Share your findings with the class.

Guided Review

1. Read *Ms. Hofbart,* the chapter-opening vignette, and answer the following question.

a. What additional strategies can Ms. Hofbart use to promote the mathematics skills of her students?

After reading this chapter, you should be able to answer this as well as the following questions.

a. How can I differentiate mathematics instruction?
b. How can I differentiate science and social studies instruction?

How Can I Differentiate Mathematics Instruction?

2. The National Council of Teachers of Mathematics (NCTM) established guidelines that promote five general mathematical goals for all students. List these goals.

a. _____
_____
_____

b. _____
_____
_____

c. _____
_____
_____

d. _____
_____
_____

e. _____
_____
_____

3. This chapter offers strategies for differentiating mathematics instruction. Discuss one of the strategies under each of the following sub-headings.

a. Use a Problem-Solving Approach:

_____

_____

_____

_____

_____

b. Present Mathematics Appropriately:

_____

_____

_____

_____

_____

c. Use Teaching Aids:

_____

_____

_____

_____

_____

d. Use a Variety of Instructional Approaches:

_____

_____

_____

_____

_____

e. Help Students Develop Their Math Facts and Computation Skills:

_____

_____

_____

_____

f. Provide Feedback and Use Assessment to Guide Future Teaching:

_____

_____

_____

_____

_____

How Can I Differentiate Science and Social Studies Instruction?

4. Discuss five of the strategies presented in the textbook for differentiating science and social studies instruction.

a. _____
_____
_____
_____

b. _____
_____
_____
_____

c. _____
_____
_____
_____

d. _____
_____
_____
_____

e. _____
_____
_____
_____

Application Exercise for Chapter 11

Read "What Would You Do In Today's Diverse Classroom?" and answer the following questions.

a. What would you do to help Felicia learn mathematics?

b. What would you do to help Felicia learn science and social studies?

c. What resources and support from others would be helpful to you in helping Felicia learn mathematics, science and social studies?

d. Which study guide(s) are easiest for you to develop?

e. Which one(s) would your students like the best?

f. Which one(s) would be most effective?

Reflective Exercises for Chapter 11

1. How is this textbook organized to present information? What strategies does the author use to highlight information? What aspects of the textbook help promote student learning?

2. Look back at the notes you have taken for the textbook. What note-taking strategies did you employ? How well do you use them? Which note-taking strategies do you find to be most efficient?

3. Develop a graphic organizer, concept teaching routine, anticipation guide, or semantic web for the content presented in this chapter.

4. Select a content area and create literal, inferential, and critical questions. Share and critique your questions with a partner.

For Your Information

1. Patton, Cronin, Bassett and Koppel (1997) offer guidelines and resources for focusing mathematics teaching on the real-life demands of adulthood.

2. Midkiff and Cramer (1993) and Hopkins (1993) provide lists of children's books that relate language arts instruction and students' experiences to mathematics.

3. De la Cruz, Cage, and Lian (2000) offer examples of multicultural games to teach mathematics.

4. Mitchell, Baab, Campbell-LaVoie, and Prion (1992) have developed the Mathematics of the Environment Curriculum that teaches math by having students apply it to environmental issues in different countries using actual information about population, food, energy, and cultural factors.

5. Brosnan (1997) describes a variety of geoboard activities that you can use to teach.

6. Choate (1990) and Karrison and Carroll (1991) offer guidelines for teaching students the steps necessary for solving word problems, including studying the problem, devising checklists, identifying clues and key words, and illustrating problems.

7. Successful self-instruction techniques for teaching computation skills include equal additions (Sugai & Smith, 1986), count-bys (Lloyd, Saltzman, & Kauffman, 1981), touch math (Miller, Miller, Wheeler, & Selinger, 1989), count-ons, zero facts, doubles, and turn around (Jones, Thornton, & Toohey, 1985).

8. Miller et al. (1996) offer examples of acronym mnemonics that can be used to help students solve word problems.

9. Harmon, Katims, and Whittington (1999) developed the Person-Event-Place (PEP) strategy to help students learn to use social studies textbooks.

10. Ellis (1996) developed SNIPS, and Barry, cited in Ellis and Lenz (1987), developed the *Reading Visual Aids Strategy (RVAS)* to help students gain information from visual aids and graphic presentations.

11. Higgins, Boone, and Lovitt (1996) describe the use and effectiveness of hypermedia-developed study guides.

12. Boudah, Lenz, Bulgren, Schumaker, and Deshler (2000) offer guidelines for using a unit organizer, an interactive content enhancement organizer.

13. Crank and Bulgren (1993) and Ellis (1994, 1997, 1998) offer illustrations of frame for hierarchical, cause-effect, compare-contrast, and sequential process graphic organizers.

14. Roberts and Kellough (1996) and Maxim (1995) offer guidelines and examples for developing and using thematic instruction.

15. Bulgren et al. (1997) have developed a recall enhancement routine that can help you plan and use mnemonic strategies to improve your students= memory.

16. Several learning strategies have been developed to help students learn to use the key word method, including LINCS and IT FITS (Hughes, 1996; Lebzelter & Nowacek, 1999).

17. Greene (1994) describes a variety of mnemonic strategies to help students improve their spelling, word recognition, reading comprehension, mathematics, and study skills.

18. Coleman (1997) provides a list of companies that produce software simulation of science experiments.

19. Savage and Armstrong (1996) and Trowbridge and Bybee (1996) offer descriptions and examples of how instructional techniques and multimedia can be used to teach science and social studies.

20. Ebenezer and Lau (1999) offer guidelines for using the Internet to teach science and appropriate websites.

SELF-TEST FOR CHAPTER 11

Directions: Select the best answer for each question. Try to answer each question, even though you might be unsure of the best answer. Remember that this is a practice test. You will not be penalized for guessing. However, before you take your class examinations, you should clarify with the instructor whether you will be penalized for guessing.

1. Which is **not** one of the five general mathematics goals of the National Council of Teachers of Mathematics?
   a. Learning to value mathematics
   b. Learning to communicate linguistically
   c. Becoming mathematical problem solvers
   d. Learning to reason mathematically

2. Which of the following uses humor to explain that students encounter math all the time?
   a. Tension Decontamination
   b. Math Curse
   c. Antiseptic Bouncing
   d. Math Humor

3. Which of the following calculators has the capacity to state the function or name of each key as it is pressed?
   a. Speech Plus Calculator
   b. Bart's Pet Calculator
   c. Higgins Calculator
   d. Amazing Calculator

4. MiC is a middle school math curriculum designed to teach:
   a. Numbers
   b. Algebra
   c. Probability and statistics
   d. All of the above

5. Which of the following might Mr. Gonzales use to develop students' word problem-solving skills?
   a. Teach students to differentiate between relevant and irrelevant information
   b. Encourage students to estimate answers and brainstorm solutions to word problems
   c. Give students problems that have more than one answer
   d. All of the above

6. A student is having difficulty remembering the sequence of operations in performing long division. A teacher could help this student remember the sequence by using:
   a. Manipulatives
   b. Flip charts
   c. Graph paper
   d. All of the above

7. Which of the following factors can affect students' ability to solve word problems?
   a. Syntactical complexity
   b. Sequence
   c. Number of ideas presented
   d. All of the above

8. Prior to reading a textbook selection, Ms. Shand discusses with students the answers to a series of true or false statements and questions relating to the material in the selection. Ms. Shand is using a/an:
   a. Concept teaching routine
   b. Anticipation guide
   c. Keyword method
   d. Semantic web

9. Ms. Livingstone wants to use a graphic organizer to help her students understand and remember cause-effect information. What type of graphic organizer should she use?
   a. Central graphic organizer
   b. Hierarchical graphic organizer
   c. Directional graphic organizer
   d. Comparative graphic organizer

10. A student is using the sentence, Every Good Boy Deserves Fun" to remember a list of terms. The student is using:
    a. Mnemonics
    b. Mental visualization
    c. Pegword Method
    d. Chunking

True or False Questions

Directions: Read each statement carefully. Circle true if the answer is true, and false if the answer is false.

11. You can use rhythms, songs, raps, and chants to teach mathematics.
    True   False

12. Manipulatives and concrete teaching aids can be used to promote students' understanding of abstract and symbolic concepts.
    True   False

13. Instructional technology has **not** been found useful in supporting mathematics instruction.
    True   False

14. Students with emotional and behavioral disorders are most likely to have difficulty solving mathematics word problems.
    True   False

15. These patterns are typically used by authors to present content: enumeration, time order, compare-contrast, cause-effect, and problem solution.
    True   False

Sentence Completion Questions

16. Central and _____ graphic organizers are structured around one central topic.

17. A diagram that includes a key word or phrase that relates to the main point of the content is referred to as a _____.

18. The _____ is an advanced organizer that introduces students to new content by having them respond to several oral or written statements.

19. Ms. Douglas uses questions that require her students to provide answers that are not explicitly stated in the reading passage. She is using _____ _____.

20. The learning cycle begins with the _____.

Essay Questions

21. Discuss the steps teachers should follow in using manipulatives to teach math concepts.

22. How can teachers use math journals to enhance students' math skills?

23. How can calculators assist students in developing their math skills? What is a talking calculator?

24. Identify and describe three different types of study guides. Discuss the steps you would use to develop one of these types of study guides.

Matching Questions

Match the type of student error with its instructional strategy.

Instructional Strategy	Student Error
1. _____ Use manipulatives, concrete materials, and pictorial displays.	A. Step in algorithm has been omitted
2. _____ Teach students a self-monitoring strategy to check that all steps have been completed.	B. Placement error
3. _____ Give students opportunities to practice the rule.	C. Regrouping error
4. _____ Break down the task into smaller and simpler units.	D. Conceptual misunderstandings

Chapter 12: Evaluating the Effectiveness of Inclusion

Chapter Overview

Chapter twelve provides a framework and specific strategies and resources for evaluating inclusion programs. Specifically, it presents guidelines for determining if your inclusion program is resulting in positive educational, social, behavioral, and self-concept outlines for all of your students. It also provides techniques for examining family members' and educators' perceptions of and experiences with inclusion that can help you assess your students' progress and evaluate various programmatic components of your inclusion program.

Chapter Objectives

Upon completion of this chapter, students should be able to:

1. Use a variety of informal and formal testing procedures to evaluate the academic performance of students.
2. Use a variety of alternative grading systems.
3. Adapt teacher-made tests to assess students' performance.
4. Use a variety of alternative testing techniques to help students perform at their optimal level.
5. Teach students to use a variety of test-taking skills.
6. Involve parents, teachers, and students in evaluating students' progress.
7. Evaluate the social and behavioral performance of students.
8. Measure students', parents', teachers', and family members' perceptions of inclusion programs.
9. Understand how to improve the effectiveness of their inclusion programs.

Chapter Outline

I.   *Ms. Charles and Ms. Mackey* (Chapter-opening vignette)
II.   How Can I Evaluate the Academic Performance of Students?
    1.   Standardized Testing
        a. Types of Standardized Tests
            i. Norm-Referenced Testing
            ii. Criterion-Referenced Testing
        b. Testing Accommodations for Diverse Learners
            i.   Presentation of Items and Directions
            ii. Responses to Items
            iii. Scheduling and Setting Alternatives
            iv. Test Adaptations for Second Language Learners

Training Prior to Testing
2. Alternatives to Standardized Testing
   a. Curriculum-Based Measurement
   b. Authentic/Performance Assessment
   c. Portfolio Assessment
   d. Rubrics
   e. Technology-Based Testing
   f. Dynamic Assessment
   g. Observations
   h. Teacher-Made Tests
      i. Test Content
      ii. Multiple-Choice Items
      iii. Matching Items
      iv. True-False Items
      v. Sentence Completion Items
      vi. Essay Questions
      vii. Readability of Items
      viii. Scoring
      ix. Cooperative Group Testing
      x. Student Involvement
3. Gathering Additional Information About the Academic Progress of Diverse Learners
   a. Error Analysis
   b. Think-Alouds
   c. Student Journals/Learning Logs
   d. Self-Evaluation Questionnaires/Interviews
4. Reporting Information About the Academic Progress of Diverse Learners
   a. IEPs
   b. Report Card Grades
      i. Alternative Grading Systems

III. How Can I Evaluate the Social and Behavioral Performance of Students?
1. Observational Techniques
2. Sociometric Techniques
3. Self-Concept Measures

IV. How Can I Measure Perceptions of My Inclusion Program?
1. Students' Perceptions
2. Teachers' Perceptions
   a. Questionnaires
   b. Interviews
   c. Journals
3. Family Members' Perceptions
4. Interviews and Questionnaires

V. How Can I Improve the Effectiveness of My Inclusion Program?
1. Examine the Impact on Student Performance
2. Determine Program Strengths, Concerns, and Possible Solutions

Chapter Summary

This chapter offered educators a variety of strategies for evaluating the progress of students in inclusive settings. Keep the following questions in mind as you review this chapter.

a. How Can I Evaluate the Academic Performance of Students?
b. How Can I Evaluate the Social and Behavioral Performance of Students?
c. How Can I Measure Perceptions of My Inclusion Program?
d. How Can I Improve the Effectiveness of My Inclusion Program?

Key Terms

Norm-referenced testing

Criterion-referenced testing

Curriculum-based measurement

Authentic/Performance assessment

Portfolio assessment

Rubrics

Technology-based testing

Dynamic assessment

Alternate grading systems

Sociometric techniques

Self-concept measures

Inclusion

Learning Activities

1. Work in a small cooperative learning group to design an evaluation plan to assess the progress of a student. The plan should describe the use of assessment procedures, interviews, observations, and monitoring techniques. Ask each group to share its plan with the class.

2. Develop a criterion-referenced test.

3. Design and conduct a curriculum-based measurement and a portfolio assessment with a student over a period of several weeks. Present your product and discuss your results with the class.

4. Work with three classmates to identify appropriate performance assessment tasks for various content areas. Share your performance assessment tasks with the class.

5. As a member of a small cooperative group, select a student project and create a rubric for that project. Share your rubric with the class.

6. Administer the sample inclusion surveys developed by the author (Figures 12.9 and 12.10 in the textbook) to examine the experiences of students in inclusive classrooms. Analyze and share your findings with the class.

7. Administer the sample teacher's inclusion survey developed by the author (Figure 12.11 in the textbook) to examine the experiences of general and special education teachers who teach in inclusive classrooms. Analyze and share your findings with the class. You could also administer the sample interview questions in Figure 12.12 to examine the experiences of educators working in inclusive classrooms.

Learning Activities

1. Divide the class into small groups. Ask each group to design an evaluation plan to assess the progress of a student. The plan should describe the use of assessment procedures, interviews, observations, and monitoring techniques. Ask each group to share its plan with the class.

2. Divide the class into small groups. Ask each group to develop a criterion-referenced test.

3. Ask each student to design and conduct a curriculum-based measurement and a portfolio assessment with a student over a period of several weeks. Ask each student to present their products and discuss their results with the class.

4. Divide the class into small groups. Ask each group to identify appropriate performance assessment tasks for various content areas. Have each group share their performance assessment tasks with the class.

5. Divide the class into small groups. Ask each group to select a student project and create a rubric for that project. Have each group share their rubric with the class.

6. Divide the class into small groups. Ask each group to create three caption statement prompts. Have each group share their prompts with the class.

7. Divide the class into small groups. Ask each group to produce three examples of error patterns students might make in performing a task. Ask each group to write their examples on the blackboard so that the rest of the class can perform an error analysis on each example to identify the error pattern that is being depicted.

8. Ask students to interview teachers concerning the grading systems they use and their reactions to these systems. Asks students to discuss their findings with the class.

9. Divide the class into small groups. Provide each group with some information about students. Based on this information, ask the groups to design various alternative grading systems. Ask each group to share their work with the class.

10. Discuss the following questions with the class: (a) Should students with disabilities be graded using the same grading systems as their peers? (b) Should grades be assigned to students with disabilities only by their general education teachers?

11. Divide the class into small groups. Give each group a textbook relating to a content area or grade they would like to teach. Using the content in the textbook, ask each group to design a test that includes multiple choice, true/false, matching, sentence completion and essay items. The groups should use the information presented in Figure 12.9 to guide them in adapting the content and format of the test for students. Ask the group to delineate the ways they would adapt the test for second language learners. Ask each group to share their tests with the class.

12. Ask students to interview teachers concerning the use of alternative testing techniques. Ask the students to share their findings with the class.

13. Discuss the following questions with the class. Do alternative testing techniques give students with disabilities an advantage over other students? Do alternative testing techniques violate the integrity of tests?

14. Prior to discussing test taking skills, give students a sample test and have them discuss the test-taking skills they used during the sample test.

15. Invite local educators and a member of the state education department to discuss state and local requirements and alternatives for students with disabilities concerning large scale and statewide testing and graduation requirements.

16. Administer the sample inclusion surveys developed by the author (Figures 12.9 and 12.10 in the textbook) to examine the experiences of students in inclusive classrooms. Analyze and share your findings with the class.

17. Administer the sample teacher's inclusion survey developed by the author (Figure 12.11 in the textbook) to examine the experiences of general and special education teachers who teach in inclusive classrooms. Analyze and share your findings with the class. You could also administer the sample interview questions in Figure 12.12 to examine the experiences of educators working in inclusive classrooms or the sample interview questions in Figures 12.14 and 12.15 to examine the perceptions of families concerning inclusion programs.

Guided Review

1. Read *Ms. Charles and Ms. Mackey*, the chapter-opening vignette and answer the following question.

a. How can Ms. Charles and Ms. Mackey evaluate the effectiveness of their inclusion program?

After reading this chapter, you should be able to answer this as well as the following questions.

a. How can I evaluate the academic performance of students?
b. How can I evaluate the social and behavioral performance of students?
c. How can I measure perceptions of my inclusion program?
d. How can I improve the effectiveness of my inclusion program?

How Can I Evaluate the Academic Performance of Students?

2. Define the following types of standardized tests.

a. Norm-Referenced Testing

_____

_____

_____

_____

b. Criterion-Referenced Testing

_____

_____

_____

_____

3. Discuss three of the following testing accommodations for diverse learners.
   Presentation of Items and Directions
   Responses to Items
   Scheduling and Setting Alternatives
   Test Adaptations for Second Language Learners
   Training Prior to Testing

_____

_____

_____

_____

_____
_____
_____
_____
_____
_____
_____
_____

4. Briefly discuss each of the following alternatives to standardized testing.

a. Curriculum-Based Measurement

_____
_____
_____
_____

b. Authentic/Performance Assessment

_____
_____
_____
_____

c. Portfolio Assessment

_____
_____
_____
_____

d. Rubrics

_____
_____
_____
_____

e. Technology-Based Testing

_____
_____
_____
_____

f. Dynamic Assessment

_____
_____

_____

_____

_____

g. Observations

_____

_____

_____

_____

h. Teacher-Made Tests

_____

_____

_____

_____

5. You can gather additional information about the academic progress of diverse learners by administering the following methods. Discuss two of the following:

a. Error Analysis
b. Think-Alouds
c. Student Journals/Learning Logs
d. Self-Evaluation Questionnaires/Interviews

_____

_____

_____

_____

_____

_____

_____

_____

6. Discuss the following strategies that can be used for reporting information about the academic progress of diverse learners.

a. IEPs

_____

_____

_____

_____

b. Report Card Grades

_____

_____

_____

_____

How Can I Evaluate the Social and Behavioral Performance of Students?

7. You can use the following to evaluate the social and behavioral performance of students. Discuss each.

a. Observational Techniques

_____
_____
_____
_____

b. Sociometric Techniques

_____
_____
_____
_____

c. Self-Concept Measures

_____
_____
_____
_____

How Can I Measure Perceptions of My Inclusion Program?

8. List four strategies that you can use to measure perceptions of inclusion programs.

a.
b.
c
d.

How Can I Improve the Effectiveness of My Inclusion Program?

9. Briefly discuss how you could use the data on the perceptions of students, teachers, and family members regarding inclusion programs.

_____
_____
_____
_____
_____

Application Exercise For Chapter 12

Read "What Would You Do in Today's Diverse Classroom" and answer the following questions.

a. What would be the goals of your inclusion program for these students?

b. How would you evaluate the effectiveness of your inclusion program on the academic, behavioral, and social performance of these students?

c. Would you include these students in your school=s statewide and districtwide testing program? If yes, what testing accommodations might they need? If no, what alternative assessment techniques would you use to assess their progress?

d. What roles would the perceptions of students, educators, and family members perform in your evaluation of the effectiveness of your inclusion program? How would you gather information from these groups about your inclusion program?

e. How would you assess your perceptions of your inclusion program?

f. What difficulties might arise in educating these students in your inclusion program? How could you address these difficulties to improve the effectiveness of your inclusion program?

Reflective Exercise for Chapter 12

1. What is your view of the inclusion of students with disabilities in statewide assessments? How will it affect them, you, and your school district?

2. Do alternative testing techniques give students with disabilities an advantage over other students? Would alternative testing techniques violate the integrity of tests?

3. What studying and test-taking strategies do you use? Are they successful? How did you learn these strategies?

4. What performance/authentic assessment tasks might be appropriate for measuring your understanding of the material presented in this course and book.

5. You applied for a job in a local school district by sending a resume and a letter of interest. The superintendent's office asks you to come in for an interview and bring a portfolio representing your experiences and training. What items would you include in the portfolio? How would you organize and present them?

6. Do grading alternatives and accommodations compromise standards and course

integrity? Should grades be assigned only by the general education classroom teacher or through collaboration with others?

For Your Information

1. Lachat (1997) provides guidelines for examining the appropriateness of large-scale tests for students from various cultural and language backgrounds.

2. Elliott, Kratochwill, and Schulte (1998) developed the Assessment Accommodation Checklist and Fuchs, Karns, Eaton, and Hamlett (1999) developed the Dynamic Assessment of Test Accommodations (DATA) to help teachers select testing accommodations for students with a wide range of disabilities.

3. Fradd and Wilen (1990) provide guidelines for using interpreters and translators to assess the test performance of second language learners.

4. Hughes, Deshler, Ruhl, and Schumaker (1993) improved students' test performance by teaching them to use *PIRATES: P*repare to succeed; *I*nspect the instructions; *R*ead, remember, reduce; *A*nswer or abandon; *T*urn back; *E*stimate; *S*urvey. Hughes (1996) developed *ANSWER*, an essay test-taking learning strategy that involves the following steps: *A*nalyze the situation; *N*otice requirements; *S*et up an outline; *W*ork in details; *E*ngineer your answer; and *R*eview your answer.

5. Idol, Nevin, & Paolucci-Whitcomb (1999) and Paulsen (1997) offer guidelines and models for using CBM to assess student performance in inclusive classrooms.

6. Wiggins (1997) and Herman, Aschbacher, and Winters (1992) provide questions that can guide you in selecting appropriate performance/authentic assessment tasks.

7. States like Kentucky have established an alternate portfolio assessment system to involve students with moderate and severe cognitive disabilities in statewide testing system (Kearns, Kleinert, & Kennedy, 1999).

8. Gelfer and Perkins (1998) and O=Malley & Valdez Pierce (1996) provide guidelines for developing portfolios with young children, and with students from culturally and linguistically diverse backgrounds, respectively.

9. Jochum, Curran, and Reetz (1998) outline the roles of students, family members, general and special educators, and ancillary support personnel in the portfolio process.

10. Countryman and Schroeder (1996) and Hebert and Schultz (1996) offer suggestions for helping students share their portfolios at conferences with their teachers and

families, and Graham and Fahey (1999) describe how a collaborative assessment conference is used to engage teachers in a discussion of students' work.

11. Finson and Ormsbee (1998) discuss and give examples of the use of rubrics in inclusive classrooms.

12. Test development software programs to help you in creating your own tests are available (Bahr & Bahr, 1997).

13. Cristiansen and Vogel (1998) offer a decision making model that teachers working collaboratively in inclusive classrooms can use to determine appropriate grading systems for student with disabilities.

14. The *Educational Assessment of Social Interaction (EASI)* (Hunt, Alwell, Farron-Davis, & Goetz, 1996), the *Interactive Partnership Scale (IPS)* (Hunt, Alwell, Farron-Davis, & Goetz, 1996), *Social Interaction Checklist (SIC)* (Kennedy, Shukla, & Fryxell, 1997), *Social Contact Assessment Form* (Kennedy, Shukla, & Fryxell, 1997), and the *School-Based Social Network Form* (Kennedy, Shukla, & Fryxell, 1997) can assist you in recording and categorizing your observations of student interactions.

15. Bryan (1997) offers examples of assessment instruments designed to assess students= affective status, self-efficacy, social status, and social skills.

16. Bogdan and Biklen (1992) offer guidelines for interviewing students

SELF-TEST FOR CHAPTER 12

Directions: Select the best answer for each question. Try to answer each question, even though you might be unsure of the best answer. Remember that this is a practice test. You will not be penalized for guessing. However, before you take your class examinations, you should clarify with the instructor whether you will be penalized for guessing.

1. Which of the following statements is **false** concerning norm-referenced testing? Norm-referenced tests can:
    a. Be used to determine whether or not a student should have a more extensive evaluation
    b. Provide information as to whether a student is eligible for special education services
    c. Provide educators with information on the specific skills that a student has mastered
    d. Help educators determine curricular areas in which students excel or need remedial instruction

2. Adaptations in testing administration and procedures will be needed for some diverse learners. These testing accommodations also are referred to as:
    a. Alternative testing techniques
    b. Norm-referenced techniques
    c. Criterion-referenced techniques
    d. All of the above

3. A student portfolio that shows changes in the products and process associated with learning throughout a period of time is referred to as a:
    a. Show case portfolio
    b. Goal-based portfolio
    c. Cumulative portfolio
    d. Complete portfolio

4. Brief descriptions that identify a portfolio item, its date, and the context in which the items were produced are referred to as:
    a. Caption statements
    b. Summary statements
    c. Rubrics
    d. Reflective statements

5. Which statement is **true** about designing matching test questions for students?
   a. There should be an equal number of entries in the two columns
   b. The longer statement should be in the column on the left
   c. The matching activity should have more than 10 pairs
   d. The directions should be on a separate page

6. Which of the following is a strategy to modify multiple choice questions for students?
   a. Reduce the number of response choices
   b. Eliminate choices such as "all of the above," and "none of the above"
   c. Allow students to circle the correct answer
   d. All of the above

7. Information on the strategies students use to approach a task can be obtained through use of:
   a. Norm-referenced testing
   b. Minimum competency testing
   c. Criterion-referenced testing
   d. Think-aloud techniques

8. An alternative grading system that measures student progress by use of performance measures on pretests and posttests is:
   a. Multiple grading
   b. Level grading
   c. Shared grading
   d. Mastery level/criterion systems

9. A student receives a grade of B4, which indicates that the student is working in the B range at the fourth grade level. This is an example of:
   a. Level grading
   b. Shared grading
   c. Student self-comparison
   d. Descriptive grading

10. The teachers in the seventh grade decide that students should receive grades for ability, effort, and achievement in each class. This grading alternative is an example of:
    a. Shared grading
    b. Multiple grading
    c. Level grading
    d. None of the above

True or False Questions

Directions: Read each statement carefully. Circle true if the answer is true, and false if the answer is false.

11. A reader would be an appropriate modification for a student taking a math test that requires considerable reading.
    True   False

12. Portfolios are student-centered and archival in nature.
    True   False

13. You do **not** need to modify tests for second language learners and those who speak vernacular dialects.
    True   False

14. Prior to testing, you can allow your students to practice taking tests.
    True   False

15. You can incorporate students' suggestions in writing and scoring tests.
    True   False

Sentence Completion Questions

16. _____ provides individualized direction and repeated measures of students' proficiency and progress in the curriculum.

17. Authentic/performance assessment and portfolio assessment include the use of _____, statements specifying the criteria associated with different levels of proficiency for evaluating student performance.

18. In _____, students state the processes they are using and describe their thoughts while working on a task.

19. _____ should be careful not to give students cues and additional information that may affect their performance on tests.

20. In _____, students work collaboratively on open-ended tasks that have non-routine solutions.

Essay Questions

21. Identify and discuss ways a teacher could design the format of a test to address the unique needs of students with reading problems and students with organizational problems.

22. Describe how you would implement four of the following alternative grading systems:

Individualized Education Program	Multiple Grading
Contract Grading	Level Grading
Pass/Fail Systems	Shared Grading
Mastery Level/Criterion Systems	Descriptive Grading
Checklists and Rating Scales	

23. Describe three ways a teacher could improve the readability of items on a test.

24. Discuss the steps you would use to develop a rubric.

25. How can teachers make their tests fairer by involving students in the grading process?

Matching Questions

Match the type of student error with its instructional strategy.

Description	Alternative to Standardized Testing
1. _____ They are student-centered and archival in nature	A. Curriculum-Based Measurement
2. _____ Learning activities are not only meaningful, complex, and relevant but are incorporated into the assessment process.	B. Authentic/Performance Assessment
3. _____ It provides individualized, direct and repeated measures of students' proficiency and progress in the curriculum.	C. Portfolio Assessment
4. _____ Students create and make things.	
5. _____ Students, teachers, and family members are involved in creating a continuous and purposeful collection of various authentic student products.	
6. _____ It links testing, teaching, and evaluation.	

Answers for Chapter 1 Self-Test

Multiple Choice Questions

1.1 B (pp. 5–6)	1.5 A (p. 16)	1.9 B (p. 20)	1.13 D (p. 29)
1.2 B (p. 12)	1.6 C (p. 17)	1.10 A (p. 21)	1.14 A (pp. 31–32)
1.3 D (p. 13)	1.7 C (p. 18)	1.11 A (p. 22)	
1.4 B (p. 15)	1.8 A (p. 13)	1.12 B (p. 23)	

True or False Questions

1.15 T (p. 11)	1.18 F (p. 15)	1.21 T (pp. 12–13)	1.24 T (p. 25)
1.16 T (p. 11)	1.19 T (p. 20)	1.22 F (p. 22)	
1.17 T (p. 11)	1.20 T (p. 11)	1.23 F (p. 24)	

Sentence Completion Questions

1.25 deinstitutionalization	(p. 14)
1.26 Inclusion	(p. 5)
1.27 normalization	(p. 14)
1.28 separate educational facilities are inherently unequal	(p. 15)
1.29 least restrictive environment	(p. 11)

Matching Questions

1.1 E (p. 11)	1.4 G (p. 13)	1.7 J (p. 13)	1.10 H (p. 13)
1.2 C (p. 11)	1.5 B (p. 13)	1.8 F (p. 13)	
1.3 I (pp. 12–13)	1.6 D (p. 13)	1.9 A (p. 13)	

Answers for Chapter 2 Self-Test

Multiple Choice Questions

2.1 D (p. 38)	2.5 A (p. 53)	2.9 A (p. 57)	2.13 A (p. 70)
2.2 D (pp. 38–47)	2.6 B (p. 54)	2.10 C (p. 59)	2.14 B (p. 73)
2.3 D (pp. 50–51)	2.7 B (p. 54)	2.11 D (p. 60)	
2.4 C (p. 52)	2.8 B (p. 56)	2.12 C (p. 61)	

True or False Questions

2.15 T (pp. 49–50)	2.18 F (p. 56)	2.21 F (p. 54)	2.24 T (p. 65)
2.16 F (p. 50)	2.19 F (p. 54)	2.22 T (p. 59)	
2.17 T (p. 52)	2.20 F (pp. 50–51)	2.23 T (p. 62)	

Sentence Completion Questions

2.25	transition	(p. 46)
2.26	Ataxia	(p. 59)
2.27	decibels, hertz	(p. 70)
2.28	Receptive	(p. 56)
2.29	Spina bifida	(p. 59)

Matching Questions

2.1 B (p. 67)	2.5 B (p. 67)
2.2 D (p. 68)	2.6 A (p. 67)
2.3 C (p. 68)	2.7 D (p. 68)
2.4 A (p. 67)	2.8 C (p. 68)

Answers for Chapter 3 Self-Test

Multiple Choice Questions

3.1 D (p. 78)	3.6 D (p. 86)	3.11 A (p. 104)
3.2 A (p. 79)	3.7 A (p. 87)	3.12 D (p. 107)
3.3 C (p. 80)	3.8 C (p. 91)	3.13 A (p. 111)
3.4 D (p. 81)	3.9 B (p. 92)	
3.5 D (p. 81)	3.10 D (p. 93)	

True or False Questions

3.14 T (p. 79)
3.15 T (p. 81)
3.16 F (p. 87)
3.17 T (p. 89)
3.18 T (p. 109)

Sentence Completion Questions

3.19 bilingual	(p. 88)
3.20 30	(p. 80)
3.21 migrant workers **or** Native Americans	(p. 82) and (p. 84) respectively
3.22 suburbs	(p. 84)
3.23 two-way	(p. 88)

Matching

3.1 A	3.5 F
3.2 H	3.6 E
3.3 G	3.7 D
3.4 B	3.8 C

The answers to the matching questions are on page 97.

Answers for Chapter 4 Self-Test

Multiple Choice Questions

4.1 D (p. 120)	4.5 C (p.125)	4.9 C (p. 128)
4.2 C (p. 122)	4.6 D (p. 126)	4.10 C (p. 138)
4.3 A (p. 124)	4.7 B (p. 127)	4.11 D (p. 145)
4.4 D (p. 124)	4.8 D (p. 130)	

True or False Questions

4.12 F (p. 121)	4.16 F (p. 128)	4.20 T (p. 143)
4.13 T (p.124)	4.17 F (p. 131)	4.21 F (p. 136)
4.14 T (p. 126)	4.18 F (p. 138)	
4.15 F (p. 126)	4.19 T (p.141)	

Sentence Completion Questions

4.22 comprehensive planning team	(p.120)
4.23 school administrator	(p. 120)
4.24 School physicians	(p. 124)
4.25 Families	(p. 145)
4.26 acculturation	(p. 145)

Matching Question

4.1 E (p. 138)
4.2 B (p. 127)
4.3 C (p. 128)
4.4 A (p 126)
4.5 D (p. 138)

Answers for Chapter 5 Self-Test

Multiple Choice Questions

5.1 C (p. 163)	5.5 D (p. 185)	5.9 B (p.178)
5.2 D (p. 174)	5.6 D (p. 160)	5.10 C (p.172)
5.3 A (p. 177)	5.7 D (p. 163)	
5.4 B (p. 178)	5.8 D (p.164)	

True or False Questions

5.11 F (p. 160)	5.15 F (pp. 169–170)	5.19 T (p. 170)
5.12 F (p. 160)	5.16 T (p. 162)	5.20 F (p. 172)
5.13 F (p. 161)	5.17 T (p. 165)	
5.14 F (pp. 160–161)	5.18 F (p. 169)	

Sentence Completion Questions

5.21 sociograms   (p. 161)
5.22 attitudes   (p. 162)
5.23 hearing losses   (p. 169)
5.24 stereotypes   (p. 180)
5.25 Simulations   (pp. 165–166)

Matching Question

5.1 C (p. 174)
5.2 D (p. 177)
5.3 E (p. 180)
5.4 F (p. 183)
5.5 A (p. 163)
5.6 B (p. 165)

Answers for Chapter 6 Self-Test

Multiple Choice Questions

6.1 D (p. 192)	6.6 C (p.200)	6.11 C (p. 214)	
6.2 A (pp. 193–194)	6.7 B (p. 209)	6.12 D (p. 219)	
6.3 C (p. 194)	6.8 C (pp. 210–211)	6.13 A (p. 210)	
6.4 C (p. 194)	6.9 A (p. 216)	6.14 C (p. 209)	
6.5 D (pp. 196-197)	6.10 C (p. 210)		

True or False Questions

6.15 F (p. 192)
6.16 T (p. 193)
6.17 F (p. 194)
6.18 T (p. 201)
6.19 T (p. 204)

Sentence Completion Questions

6.20 transitions	(p. 192)
6.21 modeling	(p. 209)
6.22 competitive employment	(p. 214)
6.23 job coach	(p. 214)
6.24 attribution training	(p. 220)

Matching Question

6.1 C (p. 211)
6.2 A (p. 210)
6.3 B (p. 210)
6.4 A (p. 210)

Answers for Chapter 7 Self-Test

Multiple Choice Questions

7.1 A (p. 228)   7.6 C (pp. 230–231)   7.11 C (pp. 247–248)
7.2 D (p. 229)   7.7 B (p. 232)   7.12 B (p 250)
7.3 D (p. 229)   7.8 C (p. 237)   7.13 D (pp. 256–257)
7.4 C (p. 229)   7.9 B (p. 237)   7.14 B (p. 257)
7.5 D (p. 230)   7.10 B (p. 244)

True or False Questions

7.15 F (p. 232)   7.20 T (p. 238)
7.16 F (p. 244)   7.21 T (p. 239)
7. 17 T (p. 228)   7.22 F (p. 242)
7.18 F (p. 235)   7.23 F (pp. 246–247)
7.19 F (p 237)

Sentence Completion Questions

7.24 Event recording   (p. 230)
7.25 Values clarification   (p. 237)
7.26 Life Space Interviewing   (p. 237)
7.27 Consequence-based intervention   (p. 246)
7.28 contract   (p. 247)

Matching Question

7.1 A (p. 248)
7.2 C (p. 250)
7.3 B (p. 249)
7.4 D (p. 249)

Answers for Chapter 8 Self-Test

Multiple Choice Questions

8.1 B (p. 274)	8.6 D (p. 279)	8.11 C (p. 283)
8.2 B (p. 275)	8.7 A (p. 279)	8.12 C (p. 300)
8.3 A (p. 274)	8.8 B (p. 280)	8.13 B (pp. 301–302)
8.4 D (p.276)	8.9 D (p. 282)	8.14 D (p. 305)
8.5 B (p.279)	8.10 A (p. 282)	

True or False Questions

8.15 F (p. 274)
8.16 T (p. 274)
8.17 T (p. 290)
8.18 T (p. 303
8.19 F (p.306)

Sentence Completion Questions

8.20	locus of control	(p. 274)
8.21	treatment acceptability	(p. 278)
8.22	Postquestions	(p. 281)
8.23	verbal rehearsal	(p. 285)
8.24	parallel lessons	(p. 292)

Matching Question

8.1 C
8.2 E
8.3 A
8.4 D
8.5 B

The answers to the matching question are on page 304 of the textbook.

Answers for Chapter 9 Self-Test

Multiple Choice Questions

9.1 B (pp. 312–313)   9.5 C (p. 322)   9.9   C (p. 327)   9.13 C (p. 332)
9.2 B (p. 318)   9.6 A (p. 319)   9.10 C (p. 333)   9.14 D (p. 314)
9.3 A (p.316)   9.7 D (pp. 321–322) 9.11 D (p. 327)
9.4 D (p. 317)   9.8 A (p. 325)   9.12 B (p. 339–341)

True or False Questions

9.15 T (p. 213)   9.19 T (p. 318)   9.23 F (p. 319)
9.16 T (p. 314)   9.20 F (p. 318)   9.24 T (p. 320)
9.17 F (p. 315)   9.21 T (p. 318)
9.18 T (p. 316)   9.22 F (p. 319)

Sentence Completion Questions

9.25 Positive interdependence   (p. 333)
9.26 Task analysis   (p. 323)
9.27 Face-to-face   (p. 333)
9.28 Role delineation   (p. 339)
9.29 Contract grading   (p. 339)

Matching Questions

9.1   B (p. 318)
9.2   D (p. 318)
9.3   A (p. 318)
9.4   C (p. 319)

Answers for Chapter 10 Self-Test

Multiple Choice Questions

10.1 D (p. 348)	10.6 D (pp. 352–353)
10.2 D (p. 348)	10.7 A (p. 356)
10.3 D (p. 356)	10.8 A (p. 358)
10.4 A (p. 358)	10.9 B (p. 359)
10.5 B (p. 363)	10.10 D (p. 362–363)

True or False Questions

10.11 F (p. 349)	10.16 F (p. 356)
10.12 T (p. 348)	10.17 F (p. 356)
10.13 T (p. 348)	10.18 T (p. 357)
10.14 F (p. 349)	10.19 T (p. 366)
10.15 T (p. 352)	10.20 F (p. 364)

Sentence Completion Questions

10.21 synthetic	(p. 347)
10.22 language experience	(p. 349)
10.23 drama	(p. 353)
10.24 cooperative integrated reading and composition	(p. 354)
10.25 Multisensory strategies	(p. 355)

Matching Questions

10.1	C (p. 352)
10.2	E (p. 352)
10.3	A (p. 350)
10.4	B (p. 351)
10.5	D (p. 353)

Answers for Chapter 11 Self-Test

Multiple Choice Questions

11.1 B (p. 378)	11.6 B (p. 386)
11.2 B (p. 380)	11.7 D (p. 383)
11.3 A (p. 382)	11.8 B (p. 399)
11.4 D (p. 383)	11.9 C (p. 398)
11.5 D (p. 384)	11.10 A (p. 406)

True or False Questions

11.11 T (p. 380)
11.12 T (p. 381)
11.13 F (p. 382)
11.14 F (p. 382)
11.15 F (p. 383)

Sentence Completion Questions

11.16 hierarchical	(p. 398)
11.17 semantic web	(p. 399)
11.18 anticipation guide	(p. 399)
11.19 inferential questions	(p. 405)
11.20 engagement phase	(p. 401)

Matching Questions

11.1	C	(p. 389)
11.2	A	(p. 388)
11.3	B	(p. 389)
11.4	D	(p. 389)

Answers for Chapter 12 Self-Test

Multiple Choice Questions

12.1 C (p. 415)	12.6 D (p. 432)
12.2 A (p. 415)	12.7 D (p. 436)
12.3 C (p. 423)	12.8 D (p. 438)
12.4 A (p. 425)	12.9 A (p. 438)
12.5 B (p. 432)	12.10 B (p. 438)

True or False Questions

12.11 T (p. 415)
12.12 T (p. 415)
12.13 F (p. 417)
12.14 T (p. 418)
12.15 T (p. 436)

Sentence Completion Questions

12.16 Curriculum-based assessment	(p. 418)
12.17 rubrics	(p. 426)
12.18 think aloud techniques	(p. 436)
12.19 Proctors	(p. 416)
12.20 cooperative group testing	(p. 435)

Matching Questions

12.1   C (p. 422)
12.2   B (p. 422)
12.3   A (p. 418)
12.4   B (p. 422)
12.5   C (p. 422)
12.6   A (p. 418)